CLASSIFICATION

AND

COMMUNICATION

Classification and Communication

S R Ranganathan

SARADA RANGANATHAN ENDOWMENT
FOR LIBRARY SCIENCE
Bangalore-560 078

Shiyali Ramamrita Ranganathan (1892-1972)

Reprinted 1989
Reprint **2006**

251
J1

ISBN: 81-7000-473-X

Rs. Rs.250/-

Published By:
Ess Ess Publications
4837/24, Ansari Road,
Darya Ganj,
New Delhi-110 002
Ph.No. 23260807, 51563444, Fax: 51563334
E-mail: info@essessreference.com
url: www.essessreference.com

For:
Sarada Ranganathan Endowment for Library Science
702, 'Upstairs',
42nd Cross, III Block,
Rajajinagar,
Bangalore-560 010.
Ph.No. 23305109
E-mail: srels@vsnl.com

Printed in India at: Printline, New Delhi

To
Sow Sarada

CONTENTS

ACKNOWLEDGMENTS

The author's thanks are due to :

1. The Vice-Chancellor and the authorities of the University of Delhi for the institution of a post-graduate degree course in Library Science which has provided opportunity for continued work in the subject and for having taken up the publication of this book ;

2. The Rockefeller Foundation for the facilities provided to observe the work of several industrial libraries in U. S. A. in the summer of 1950, which added to the experience on which this book is based ;

3. Shri T. N. Koranne, B.Sc., B.Lib.Sc., for help in preparing the index ;

4. Shri P. N. Kaula, B.A., B.Lib.Sc., for help in reading the proofs ; and

5. Shri K. Mahalingam for preparing the press copy.

CONSPECTUS

The chapters fall into three groups. Those in the first octave are devoted to the evolution of the sense in which the term classification has been used. Those in the second are turned on communication. The chapters in the third octave determine the domain of classification in communication and the need for examining and strengthening the foundation of classification.

Chapter 11 refers to dichotomy and the formation of a multitude of groups in a systematic manner. Most intellectual problems are stated to turn out ultimately into problems of classification.

Chapter 12 refers to purposive arrangement as a neural necessity and shows that the efficiency of communication depends on clarity of expression and that the latter depends on the standard of classifying. It makes out a case for the introduction of training in classification in the courses of formal education and for the necessary research needed for implementing the idea.

Chapter 13 shows the necessity for representing classes by ordinal numbers in order to mechanise arrangement in a preferred order. It pictures a system of class numbers as an artificial language of ordinal numbers designed for this purpose. It then examines in succession the various notational devices made necessary when the universe of discourse becomes infinite and multiply infinite. It evaluates decimal-fraction-notation, faceted-notation and optional-facet-notation. It also deals with the need for phased-notation when the universe of discourse is formed by the interlocking of infinite universes.

Chapter 14 studies the Field of Knowledge as an interlocked, multiply-infinite dynamic universe of classes. It mentions the various modes in which specific subjects are formed, and traces the analogy of classification with linguistics, cartography, transformation, Boolean algebra, statecraft, medicine and toy-making. It finally introduces a helpful optical terminology including Phase, Facet, Focus, Basic Focus, Simple, Compound and Complex Foci, Dependent Focus, and Modes of Sharpening each type of Focus.

Chapter 15 shows that the classificationist becomes a bottleneck in enumerative classification and critically examines the Congress Classification and the Decimal Classification which are essentially enumerative in their design.

Chapter 16 describes an Analytico-Synthetic Classification in which the class number is built by

(1) first breaking down the specific subject into its fundamental constituent concepts ; then

(2) picking out from the appropriate schedule the correct number for each of these concepts ; and finally

(3) synthesising the numbers so picked out.

Its schedule of classification is shown to be truly analogous to linguistic dictionaries and its rules of classification to rules of grammar. The order of infinity of the potential vocabulary of such a classification is shown to be higher than that of an enumerative classification. A cluster of cells in the Space of Specific Subjects is shown to be mapped in the Space of Class Numbers correctly in all its details. It is shown to be like medicine compounded according to prescription rather than patent medicine like which an enumerative classification is. Lastly reference is made to its system of unscheduled mnemonics which enables a classifier to represent by correct digits every new link in a chain, as and when it is formed without waiting for the appearance of all the other co-ordinate links in its array. The Universal Decimal Classification is mentioned to be the first example of an analytico-synthetic classification. Its faults are traced to its retaining the rigid, enumerative Decimal Classification as its core and merely grafting to it an analytico-synthetic element. The dangers of its making the facets commutative are pointed out. Mention is made of the avoidance of these faults in the Colon Classification.

Chapter 17 enumerates the various uses of an Analy ico-Synthetic Classification apart from its originally intende . use for the mechanisation of arrangement. It describes how it helps classifiers to discover and enunciate the specific subject of a reading or kindred material by correct and consistent canalisation. It also describes how it can help readers and reference librarians towards an exact enunciation of the specific subject on which readers want materials.

Chapter 18 describes depth-classification and states a confession of faith. It shows that the promotion of world-wide communication needs that libraries should effect integration between readers and reading and kindred materials and for this purpose should use depth-classification.

Octave 2 is on communication and explores the spheres of human intercourse and communication where classification can play a useful part.

Chapter 21 shows how co-operative living seeks to pervade all levels—vital, mental and spiritual. It then shows how man is able to have co-operative living, at the mental level, even with his dead ancestors and how his invention of externalised memory gives him a perpetually enriching mental heritage. It next shows how the pull of co-operative living has been gradually extending the area of the territory of closed units of co-operative living from family to village, village to tribal area, and tribal area to nation. It shows how this pull is bound to take him towards one-world.

Chapter 22 examines the primary processes involved in communication, shows the place of language among them and the need for secondary techniques in effecting language-transfer and indicates the limitations in the way of reduction to one language.

Chapter 23 shows that the babel of tongues does the least harm in communication needed for commercial contact and describes the possible services of classification in world-wide commerce.

Chapter 24 shows that communication is most refractory in the field of political understanding, traces the attempts made to remove the difficulties of language in international conferences and concludes that classification will be of the least help in improving communication in this field.

Chapter 25 shows that the essence of literary communication is in its infinite number of strata of meanings and suggestion, and that classificatory language, which by definition has to admit of only one meaning and to yield it in the fullest measure at the very first contact, is incompatible with literary transfer.

Chapter 26 shows that neither natural nor classificatory language can be of use in spiritual communion.

Chapter 27 examines the aetiology, diagnosis and pathology of cultural polarity and describes the part that classification can play in the resolution of cultural conflicts, at the level of educational organisation and of understanding among adults.

Chapter 28 is on Intellectual Team-work and shows the need for such team-work for the supply of vital needs and in the organisational, mental and quasi-spiritual phases of life. It then pictures the present age as the age of communication. The emergence of periodicals and the swarm of embodied micro-units of thought is then dealt with. It concludes with an account of the part that classification has to play in planned search in the completion of communication among a team of intellectual workers.

Octave 3 is on the future of classification. It makes out a case for a thorough change in the foundation of classification and isolates several problems which need investigation and research in order to increase the expectation of life of any scheme of classification.

Chapter 31 individualises the stages in the process of communication of thought. It points out the various domains formed in it as it proceeds from the producer to the consumer. It describes the transformation which thought undergoes in each of these domains.

Chapter 32 examines each of the domains in communication to see if classification can have any part to play in it. It establishes that there is one domain in the main line of communication at the consumer's end, which classification should have all for itself. It also shows that, apart from the main line of communication, classification should be assigned to two loop-lines. In the first of them which moves towards the producer's end, it is the cataloguer that has to function. In the second loop-line which moves in the reverse direction, it is the reference librarian that has to function. In this loop-line he has to think intimately with the reader served and help him to enunciate his thought-needs in the Apupa pattern. Apupa pattern is defined. This chapter also shows that the Laws of Library Science will be better served if the domain of classification is shifted to the producer's end and recommends pre-natal classification of books as well as articles in periodicals. It also recommends the publication of catalogue cards of books and abstracts of articles in periodicals simultaneously with the books and the periodicals themselves. This would amount to pre-natal documentation.

Chapter 33 shows the need for three different time-schedules, one for geological time, another for public time and the third for private time. It also shows the impracticability of geographical schedules satisfying the Canon of Permanence and indicates the need for research to get over this difficulty.

Chapte r34, which deals with preliminary schedules, shows the hotch-potch nature of the traditional common sub-divisions most of which are based on Decimal Classification. It emphasises the need for some of the common sub-divisions to be turned to the care of Book Numbers and Sequence Numbers respectively.

Chapter 35 shows the ubiquitous nature of energy-facet. It shows that most of the immediate research in library classification should be on the designing of the primordial schedules of energy-facet, based on the subject-headings currently in use in the various fundamental and technological subjects.

Chapter 36 shows that the design of the schedule for matter-facet may have to recognise four levels of manifestation of matter—matter *qua* matter, substance, commodity at various stages of completion, artificial substance, and prefabricated commodity.

Chapter 37 deals with manifestation of personality as facets and foci. It illustrates the need for recognising various levels of manifestation and the need for designing suitable notational apparatus to suit the different levels of manifestation.

Chapter 38 is on the need for research in classification. This is shown to be caused by social pressure. It emphasises the need for empiricism. It also indicates that the laying of the foundation for a self-perpetuating scheme of classification with a long expectation of life calls for research in the Semiotic of Classification. This is a virgin field which requires intensive cultivation by a team of research workers. This chapter also shows how such a team should be constituted. It ends with an appeal to the Library Profession to give up any attitude of resistance to progress and re-thinking in the sphere of classification and to Unesco and other international organisations and Foundations to provide for research in classification.

ग्रन्थालयी सदासेवी पञ्चसूत्रीपरायणः ।
ग्रन्था अध्येतुमेते च सर्वेभ्यः स्वं स्वमाप्नुयुः ॥
अध्येतुः समयं शेषेदालयो नित्यमेव च ।
वर्धिष्णुरेष चिन्मूर्तिः पञ्चसूत्री सदा जयेत् ॥

Books are for use.
Every reader his book.
Every book its reader.
Save the time of the reader.
A library is a growing organism.

Part I

Classification and its Evolution

CHAPTER 11

First Sense—Primitive Use

111 Genesis

To classify, in the primitive sense, is to divide existents of the universe of discourse—concrete or conceptual, things or ideas—into two groups. All like ones are put into one group and the unlike ones into the other. 'Like' and 'unlike' can have meaning only in relation to an attribute—simple or complex. If possession of two legs is the attribute chosen, men and birds will fall into one group, while beasts and chairs will fall into the second. If ability to fly is the attribute chosen, birds, bats and butterflies will fall into one group, while men, beasts and bananas will fall into the other. If the study of the living bodies is the attribute chosen, biology, botany, zoology and medicine will fall into one group, while mathematics, physics, engineering and chemistry will fall into the other.

112 Dichotomy

If the number of groups formed is two and only two, the classification is dichotomic. Perhaps, to the earliest man, classification meant only dichotomy. "Citizens and slaves," "the chosen few and the heathens," and "western culture and eastern culture" are perhaps survivals of this primeval dichotomic complex.

113 Multitude of Groups

But man should soon have recognised that a universe of discourse often transcended dichotomy. He should have realised that the chosen attribute may be shared by existents in varying degrees or measures giving rise to many groups. This he would have got by choosing more generalised attributes. For example, if instead of 'two legs,' 'number of legs' is chosen as the attribute, groups like 'no leg,' 'one leg,' 'two legs,' 'three legs' . . . 'myriopod,' will arise. If the attribute chosen is 'height,' each of the categories 'buildings,' 'men' and 'mountains' will fall into several groups. If the attribute chosen is 'density' or 'specific heat' or 'electrical conductivity,' materials will fall into several groups. If the 'degree' is chosen as the attribute, polynomials will fall into several groups—say, linear, quadratic, cubic, bi-quadratic, quintic, sextic . . . *n*-ic. If the 'number of sides' is chosen as the attribute, rectilinear figures or polygons will fall into several groups —say, triangle, quadrangle, pentagon, hexagon . . . *n*-gon. If the 'number of faces' is chosen as the attribute, plane-faced solids or polyhedrons will fall into several groups—say, tetrahedron, pentahedron, hexahedron . . . *n*-hedron. Indeed it is a multitude of groups, which is incident in most cases. Even in the primitive stages of humanity, classification moved away from the rut of dichotomy and we may take it that classification meant division into a multitude of groups.

114 Potency

Classification, in this sense, is still highly potent, though it originated with the primitive man. It continues to take man further and further from his primitive state. Its potency increases with his increase in his power of abstraction—with the evolution of the cortex of the brain. Indeed most intellectual problems are ultimately problems of classification in the first sense.

CHAPTER 12

Second Sense—Common Use

To classify, in the second sense, is

(1) to classify in the first sense ; and

(2) to arrange the resulting groups in a preferred order. Polyhedra may be arranged in the ascending order of the number of faces; polygons, in the ascending order of the number of sides ; and polynomials, in the ascending order of the degree. For materials, the preferred order may be one of increasing density, or specific heat or electrical conductivity. When height is the attribute for classifying men, the order may be one of increasing or decreasing height ; or it may be symmetrical—say, with the tallest in the centre and those equally tall being distributed equally at equal distances on the two sides of the centre, so that the tallest man appears as the central peak. Or the central man may be the shortest so that he forms the central trough.

121 Purpose

The order preferred depends on the purpose of the arrangement. But the number of possible purposes is many. In the *Prolegomena*, the Canon of Helpful Order is mentioned as the pivot of all classification. In the *Elements*, various principles which can be used to determine helpful order are indicated. The attribute chosen to classify—the characteristic, as we call it—also depends on the purpose of the arrangement. We shall hereafter denote the preferred order among the existents of the universe of discourse by the term ' Helpful Order'.

122 Neural Necessity

To classify—to put things in some order more or less helpful, or to mention ideas in some order more or less helpful—appears to be common with man. In other words, to classify in the second sense appears to be inherent in man. Children begin to classify very early in life and the human species should also have begun to classify very early in its career. Perhaps this inherent tendency to classify—that is, to arrange in a more or less helpful order in space or time or space-time—is a concomitant of the finiteness of the speed of neural impulses in the human body. When speed is finite, structure emerges. Wherever there is structure, order emerges. When order is helpful, it is classification. The order which is thus inevitable inside the skin, so to speak, gets expressed extra-neurally also. To classify is thus a neural necessity.

123 Efficiency and Classification

Sharpness in thinking, clarity in expression, expedition in response and exactness in service depend ultimately on helpful order or good classification. The efficiency of a person is determined by the thoroughness and the helpfulness of his classifying. Some degree of efficiency may be innate in each person though it may not be the same in everybody. However, the efficiency of everybody can be increased by training in classification. One of the steps in this training is to analyse, understand and improve the process of classifying in the second sense, *i.e.*, grouping, and ranking the groups.

124 Communication and Classification

Communication is the transmitting, conveying, or exchanging of ideas, knowledge, information, etc., whether by speech, writing, signs or other symbols expressed audibly, visibly, graphically or in any other manner. Since expression is the basis of communication between man and man, efficiency of communication depends on clarity of expression. This, in its turn, depends on the standard of classifying—the standard as measured by the degree of helpfulness and the speed of performance. No doubt what is helpful will vary with the situation, the business on hand or, say, the profession. But the cortical region of the brain of man is capable of abstracting classification *qua* classification from the 'individuating particularities' of diverse situations. It enables him—nay, it drives him—to study classification in the abstract and build up a discipline of Pure Classification. This discipline will facilitate the practice of Applied Classification in any particular situation. In every sphere of life, advancement of humanity depends on the extent to which such pure disciplines are established, cultivated, and transmitted to the growing children of successive generations. If human progress depends upon communication, as communication depends on classification for its efficiency, cultivation of Pure Classification and the practice of Applied Classification become truly necessary for the advance of man.

125 Training in Classification

In the art of classifying, we have been hitherto depending largely on the innate flair of the individual.

As all are not endowed with equal flair, this dependence on flair results in inefficiency and wastage. The absence of this innate flair in some children leads, alas, to their being branded as uneducable and thrown out of schools. I remember my teacher of algebra making such summary disposal of some of my class-fellows. His test was to give a few algebraical expressions and ask the students to classify them into different groups—without any hint as to how they should be grouped. He wanted them to be sorted into non-symmetrical, symmetrical and cyclic. Many young men who could have been trained by schools to become useful members of society were outlawed because they did not have an innate flair to classify algebraic expressions in this manner—or, was it because the educational system did not realise that the capacity to classify could be cultivated by deliberate effort ? The present-day pressure of population, the unbalancing of this pressure on the one hand and the available food and other supplies and services on the other, and the demand for economy in the use of human resources, call for conscious, organised education in the art of classifying—and, for this purpose, in the science of classification in the second sense, so that deficiency in innate flair may be made up by conscious training to the necessary extent. A conscious cultivation of faculty has happened in succession in most of human activities. The time has now come for its happening in the act of classifying too.

126 Classification in Curriculum

Today classification in the second sense is assigned

to a late and hurried stage in courses on logic and scientific method elected only by a section of students. Correspondingly, it is assigned to a late, meagre, and often neglected chapter in books on logic and scentific method. This only amounts to a ritualistic recognition of its existence. It is necessary that books should be written with their main focus on classification. It is equally necessary that the rudiments of classification should be taught to children—all through by example and at the proper stage by precept also—before they leave formal schools and enter the phase of adulthood and further self-education. Improvement of communication needs this correction in curriculum in its ultimate analysis.

127 Formulation

To implement this idea, several steps will have to be taken, for the first time now. The discipline of Pure Classification should be not only established, but also formulated from this point of view. It may have to be formulated for different levels of education like elementary, intermediate and advanced. Books on this discipline should be written in different standards, with illustrations taken from diverse situations in life—that is, with bias towards different subjects—so that everybody will be able to follow it with interest. Books on teaching technique should be written setting forth the diverse methods of accustoming children to classify helpfully, the ways in which the teacher should show himself as an embodiment of its spirit and become an example worthy of imitation, the stages in which formal teaching of the discipline may be done, the quantum of theory to be done in each of the stages, and so on.

128 Research

Before such facilities can be established, considerable research should be done both in the content of the discipline of classification in the second sense and in the technique of transmitting it to growing minds. Our universities should provide for this research. They should be endowed with the men, money and opportunity needed for this research.

1291 Linear Arrangement

Arrangement—classified arrangement—which has been described as a neural necessity ultimately lands one in linear arrangement. It looks as if what may be called Poncelet's axial arrangement is what the human mind is now capable of. If it is confronted by a situation which calls for multi-dimensional arrangement, it seeks in a Cartesian manner to break it down to several linear arrangements.

1292 Multiplicity of Helpful Arrangements

Whether it is Poncelet's axial arrangement or it is arrangement based on a preliminary break-down into facets and phases; it is in all cases designed to be "helpful". The term "helpful" does not by itself uniquely determine the arrangement. For, the number of helpful arrangements of things is usually very large. This is a consequence of the number of possible arrangements—helpful or unhelpful—of *n* things being itself even very much larger. Indeed its number increases by leaps and bounds as the value of *n* increases. It is, in fact, the product of all the integers from 1 to *n*. Its value is very great and it takes long in writing. Because of this it is usual to represent it by the shorthand notation *n*.! It is referred to in speaking as 'factorial *n*'. Here is an illustrative table:

n	Possible Number of Arrangements. Factorial *n*	Order of Magnitude of Factorial *n*
1	1	10^0
2	2	10^0
3	6	10^0
4	24	10^1
5	120	10^2
6	720	10^2
7	5,040	10^3
8	40,320	10^4
9	362,880	10^5
10	3,628,800	10^6
...	...	...
17	355,687,428,096,000	10^{14}
...	...	...

Indeed the rate of growth of *n* ! is fabulously large. This means that the number of possible ways of arranging things is very, very large. In classifying, one seeks that arrangement which is helpful to the purpose for which the existents are arranged. To determine which among the innumerable arrangements is helpful to the purpose on hand is not an easy matter. But the human mind—its associative apparatus—often seizes a helpful arrangement with ease. A normal man has some instinct to do so with a fair amount of success. He is even unconscious of the very large number of arrangements from out of which he picks out one as helfpul. A superior man is one who has the flair to choose a helpful arrangement unerringly and expeditiously. Perhaps even he is often as unconscious as the normal man of the enormous number of possible arrangements he rejects instinctively. A learned man is one, the reasoning part of whose mind is so cultivated that he recognises all the factorial arrangements and relates the several arrangements to the different purposes for which they are helpful.

CHAPTER 13

Third Sense—Library Classification

To classify, in the third sense, is

(1) to classify in the second sense ; and

(2) to denote the resulting classes by ordinal numbers.

Unlike classification in the second sense, classification in the third sense is not universally practised by man. Children seldom think of denoting groups by ordinal numbers. It is not inherent in human nature to do so. To classify in the third sense, a higher order of abstraction is necessary. New centres in the cortical region of human brain have to be tapped. In the past, only a few situations have made it necessary. One of such situations arose in public libraries about the middle of last century, when

(1) many books in diverse regions of knowledge came to be added and the total stock became too unwieldy for unaided memory ; (Fifth Law) ;

(2) democracy endowed everybody with the right of free entry to libraries ; (Second Law) ;

(3) the Laws of Library Science slowly emerged introducing open-access (all the Five Laws) ; and

(4) the need arose to so organise books as to facilitate everybody finding his book and every book finding its reader with the least wastage of objective and subjective time ; (Second, Third and Fourth Laws).

In this situation some sensitive souls, among those who worked in libraries, felt the convenience that could be had by denoting specific subjects by ordinal numbers instead of by words in a natural language. It was this situation that threw forth the Decimal Classification as one of the finest and far-reaching examples of classification in the third sense. It was Melvil Dewey who brought this into vogue.

131 A Necessity

In fact, however, the use of ordinal numbers to denote classes is not merely a convenience but even a necessity, if the number of classes involved is large. As it has been seen in section 1292, the number of ways of arranging *n* classes is factorial *n*, and the rate of growth of factorial *n* is fabulously large. As a particular example we saw that the number of ways of classifying—in the third sense—17 classes is of the order of 10^{14}. Of these myriads of possible arrangements, many may be unhelpful. But no one arrangement can be singled out as the *only* helpful or even the *most* helpful one. In fact quite an appreciable number of arrangements will be equally helpful. It will be difficult to remember which one of these equally helpful arrangements we had chosen on a prior occasion. In practice, there is a greater probability for inconsistency than for consistency if we are to exercise our judgment on each occasion to choose a helpful arrangement. To state it in concrete terms, if there are 100 more or less equally helpful arrangements, the odds against our choosing the same arrangement on two different occasions are as 99 to 1 and the probability for consistency is 1/100.

The probability for our being consistent on 11 occasions is as small as 1/100,000,000,000,000,000,000. This amounts to saying that there is hardly any chance for consistency if we are to exercise our judgment about helpfulness of arrangement on each occasion. If a librarian depended on *de novo* judgment on each occasion, he will be soon landed in chaos. This will be quite apart from the time he would require to read the books on each occasion for replacing them and reading also the books in whose neighbourhood he is inclining to place them and determining their respective specific subjects.

132 Mechanisation of Arrangement

It is these considerations which add the third factor —denotation of the names of specific subjects by ordinal numbers—to the third definition of classification. If the names of the classes, in a natural language, are used to arrange them, we do not get a helpful order. In fact, names scatter classes in a most unhelpful chaotic order. It will give us an order like algebra, anger, apple, arrogance, asphalt and astronomy. The ordinal number is the symbol designed by human mind to denote order. Ordinal numbers are to be so designed that no two classes receive the same ordinal number and that the preferred arrangement is fixed once for all. If the existents of the universe of discourse are deranged, the restoration of the preferred arrangement will no longer require the judging and determining of the proper order *de novo*. All that will be needed is only a knowledge of the ordinal values of the numbers representing them. It is in this sense that we say that 'classification mechanises arrangement'.

133 Class Number

The ordinal numbers used by classification, in the third sense, to denote classes are called Class Numbers. A system of Class Numbers is called a Scheme of Classification. The following terms will be of use:

Scheme of Classification (or simply, Classification)	=A system of class numbers
Schedule of Classification (classification table)	=A dictionary giving the class numbers in their proper ordinal arrangement and showing against each class number its meaning in a natural language
Index to Classification (or simply, index)	=A dictionary giving in alphabetical order the names of classes in a natural language and showing against the name of each class its class number
Classificationist	=The person who designs a scheme of classification
To Classify (in the library sense)	=To determine the specific subject of a piece of writing or kindred material and to translate the name of the specific subject into its class number in accordance with the preferred scheme of classification
Classifier	=A person who classifies

134 Classificatory Language

The terminology introduced in the above definitions has obviously a linguistic flavour. Indeed, I hold that a system of Class Numbers does constitute an artificial language of ordinal numbers designed for the specific purpose of mechanising arrangement. We may call it a Classificatory Language. If inconsistency in arrangement is to be totally avoided, a classificatory language should have the following qualities:

(1) It should admit of no synonyms. This is equivalent to saying that no two Class Numbers should denote one and the same class.

(2) It should admit of no homonyms. This is equivalent to saying that no two classes should be denoted by one and the same Class Number.

Several of the classification schemes designed in the past have failed to possess these qualities. They have therefore led to inconsistency in arrangement. It is true to say that they failed to be classificatory languages. Those in charge of the Universal Decimal Classification today are no doubt avoiding homonyms but seem to court synonyms. This has been more fully discussed in my *Library classification and international documentation* (1948). Stray cases of synonyms occur also in the Decimal Classification. These have been pointed out in my *Library classification: Fundamentals and procedure* (1944).

135 Finite Universe

If the universe of discourse has only a finite number of existents that are all already known, it may be possible to throw them in the preferred helpful order and then represent them by the consecutive integral ordinal numbers 1, 2, 3, etc. If again the universe of discourse is finite, though all the existents may not be known at present, those that are known may be thrown into the preferred helpful order and these may be represented by integral ordinal numbers leaving liberal gaps to accommodate each of the unknown existents in the most helpful place as and when it comes to be known. Unless the Maxwellian devil of probability plays pranks, it is not likely that all the unknown existents will seek to fall into one and the same gap. However, it is a matter of experience that certain gaps get filled up more rapidly than others. The Maxwellian devil does play at least minor pranks. A gap often proves insufficient to accommodate all the true claimants to it. Whenever this happens, the classification breaks down.

136 Infinite Universe

If the number of existents is not finite, an infinity of them will ever remain unkown. As the *Vedas* say and as the modern definition of an infinite universe goes, even when we take away an infinity of existents from an infinite universe, what remains will still be infinite in number. A corollary of this is that potentially an infinity of now unknown existents may claim places between any two consecutive existents now known. This implies that each of the gaps, between two consecutive integral ordinal numbers used to denote any two consecutive existents known at present, should be separated by an infinity of integers. This is obviously an impossibility. Integers cannot therefore be used as ordinal numbers to represent the existents of an infinite universe.

1361 DECIMAL FRACTION NOTATION

The most important contribution of the Decimal Classification is the use of the decimal fraction notation to represent the existents of an infinite universe. In this notation, integers are never used. All the ordinal numbers in use are decimal fractions. When integers as well as decimal fractions are likely to occur, it is usual to distinguish them by putting a dot before decimal fractions. When only decimal fractions will occur, there is no need to put this dot as a mark of distinction. Those, whose temperament and habit does not allow them to think of a decimal fraction without a dot preceding it, may take the dot as understood before every class number in a decimal fraction notation. This facile decimal fraction notation has now been adopted by practically every well-known scheme of classification except that of the Library of Congress which persists in using the primitive method of integral notation with gaps—with all its attendant dangers including the threat of the Maxwellian devil

13611 Dot in Decimal Classification

It may be stated here as an aside that the dot which occurs after the third digit in the Decimal Classification is not a decimal point inserted to show that the number to its left is an integer and that to its right, a decimal fraction. It is used only for the superficial reason of giving relief to the eye when reading a Decimal Class Number.

13612 Generalised Ordinal Number

The fact that the numbers used in classification are always used only in the ordinal sense, implies that a scheme of classification can introduce its own ordinal numbers that have no cardinal values. The Expensive Classification, the Congress Classification, the Colon Classification and the Bibliographic Classification take advantage of this freedom and use also the letters of the alphabet in building the ordinal numbers to be used as class numbers. The Colon Classification goes still further and uses also certain punctuation marks and letters of the Greek alphabet to build its class numbers. All that is needed to exercise this freedom is that the ordinal value of each new digit introduced should be defined as lying between such and such of the existing digits.

137 Multiply Infinite Universe

We have so far seen the demands on notation made successively by

(1) finite and fully known universe ;
(2) finite but partially known universe ; and
(3) infinite universe which can be *ipso facto* only partially known.

To keep step with these, we thought respectively of

(1) notation of consecutive integers ;
(2) notation of non-consecutive integers and
(3) decimal-fraction-notation.

We shall now examine an even more complicated universe of discourse—a multiply infinite universe. Such a universe implies that infinity of existents will ever remain unknown in each of several dimensions. An existent may be found spread out in one, two, three or all dimensions. The extension of its tantacles in any one of the dimensions will result in another existent. The affiliations of an existent in such a universe may be different in different dimensions. The number of helpful arrangements among the existents of a multiply infinite universe will be even greater than in a singly infinite universe. The need for a suitable system of ordinal numbers to 'mechanise' the preferred arrangement is therefore all the greater. To match the octopus-like capacity which the existents of a multiply infinite universe have to claim immediate neighbours in several dimensions, the ordinal number chosen to represent them should have the decimal fraction quality not merely at its end, *i.e.*, after its last digit, but after each one of its digits.

1371 FACETED NOTATION

The most important contribution of the Colon Classification is the use of the faceted notation to represent the existents of a multiply infinite universe. In this notation, corresponding to each dimension in the universe of discourse, there is a zone in the class number. We use the word 'Facet' to denote at once the dimension of the universe and the corresponding zone of the class number. The ordinal numbers in most of the facets are decimal fractions —one prominent exception being what has been called Time Facet in which integers are used. The class number of any existent is multi-faceted in the measure of the latter's spread over the dimensions of the multiply infinite universe. Moreover, the number of digits in the ordinal number within any facet is in the measure of the extension of the existent in the corresponding dimension. A notational device is called for to demarcate the different zones corresponding to the different dimensions. If this notational device is given an ordinal value, the multi-faceted number formed with such devices will itself be an ordinal number.

1373 COLON CLASSFICATION

The Colon Classification owes its name to the fact that the notational device first used by it to demarcate facets in Class Number was the symbol ":" (colon). Hereafter the word 'facet' will be used instead of 'dimension' or 'zone' in accordance with the terminology of the Colon Classification.

1373 INFINITE UNIVERSE OF VARYING NUMBER OF FACETS

In the first three editions of the *Colon classification*, the implied assumption was that the number of facets in a universe of discourse is constant. Of course, among the fixed number of facets several arrangements are possible, some of which may be 'more or less helpful'. Of the 'more or less helpful' arrangements one is forcedly preferred for adoption. To mechanise the arrangement of facets in the preferred order, a rigorous face-formula is given for each universe of discourse called a Main or a Cononical class.

But it is possible to think of a universe of discourse in which the facets themselves are only partially known. As new facets come to be recognised in specific subjects in that universe and claim a particular place amidst the already known facets as the most helpful one, the notation must have a device by which this demand can be met. The existing editions of the *Colon classification* do not have such a device.

1374 OPTIONAL FACET NOTATION

The most important contribution of the investigation, now in progress in the Department of Library Science of the University of Delhi, is the use of Optional-Facet-Notation to represent existents in a multiply infinite universe the facets of whose possible specific subjects are only partially known and may be added to at any time. The results of these investigations are coming out in series in the *Annals* part of the *Abgila* (=*Annals*, *Bulletin* and *Granthalaya* of the Indian Library Association). The technique used is to recognise five genera of facets labelled facets of Time, Space, Energy (=Action, Process, Problems, etc.), Matter, and Personality—that indescribably holistic something of which the other four are attributes. These are called the Five Fundamental Categories. A distinct connecting symbol is used for each of these genera as in the following table:

Name of Facet	Connecting Symbol
Time...	. (dot)
Space	. (dot)
Energy	: (Colon)
Matter	; (semi-colon)
Personality	, (coma)

Care has been taken to see that the use of the same connecting symbol for the Time and Space Facets will not land us in difficulty. Provision is made to recognise different species in each genus. A distinct Signature Digit is being devised to go with each species. It is believed that such a functionally diversified notational apparatus will equip classification, in the third sense, to meet the demands of an infinite universe involving varying number of facets. At any rate this represents one of the possible lines of approach to the problem. In the least, it demonstrates the scope for further investigation to make library classification more efficient.

138 Universe with Loose Assemblage

Another type of possible universe of discourse which may turn up for consideration is what may be called Universe with Loose Assemblage. Two or more different universes of discourse, each infinite and self-contained in some definable sense, may have to be considered in relation to one another. We then say that the two or more universes are 'in loose assemblage' and the existent in which it is incident may be called 'Loosely Assembled existent'. A universe of existents, one at least of which is a loosely assembled existent, may be called a Universe with Loose Assemblage. Not even the faceted notation—still less the bare decimal-fraction-notation, or the bare integer notation with or without gaps—can meet the demands of a universe with loose assemblage. The later editions of the *Decimal classification* provided just one or two notational devices to meet the demands of such a universe. The Universal Decimal Classification pursued this to a greater length but it appears to have got into difficulties because of the absence of a conscious distinction between universes with loose assemblages on the one hand and multiply infinite universes on the other.

1381 PHASED NOTATION

An important contribution of the *Colon classification*, the *Library classification: Fundamentals and procedure* (1944) and the *Elements of library classification* (1946) is the isolation of the concept of Universes with Loose Assemblage. They have introduced the term 'Phase' in describing an existent which is loosely assembled. In the first edition, the *Colon classification* (1933) prescribed the digit "0" (zero) as the symbol to connect the class numbers corresponding to the constituents of an existent with loose assemblage. Of course the resulting number is itself a class number. It may be called a Phased Class Number. Each constituent of a Phased Class Number is itself a Class Number.

It must be stated here, by contrast, that all the constituents of a Faceted Class Number are not themselves class numbers.

The second edition of the *Colon classification* (1939) recognised two species of phase-relation for which it prescribed zero and colon as the respective connecting symbols. The *Fundamentals* made an objective analysis of the problem. The *Elements* isolated one more species of phase-relation. The *Abgila* has indications that the projected work in India includes a thorough analysis of phases, isolation of different species of phase-relations, and prescription of distinctive connecting symbols for them. It is hoped that this investigation will lay down a technique for handling new species of phases as an when they come to be known, though they may be unknown at present.

1391 INFINITY OF CO-ORDINATE CLASSES

What has been set forth so far may be summarised as follows :—

Infinite Hospitality in	Notational Device
Chain—to classify infinite universe calling for continued subdivision.	Decimal-fraction-notation
Facets—to classify multiply infinite universe	Faceted-notation providing for different genera and species of facets.
Phases—to classify universe with loose assemblage.	Phased-notation providing for different genera and species of phases.

A fourth problem which may arise in any infinite universe and which is comparatively simpler may now be mentioned to make the analysis complete. When we classify a universe of discourse we may land ourselves in a set of co-ordinate classes. Such a set we call, an 'Array of Classes' in contradiction to classes which are derived by a successive subdivision which we call a 'Chain of Classes.' Just as the notation provides for hospitality in chain, facets and phases, it should also provide for hospitality in array to make the classes in an array mutually exclusive and totally exhaustive of their common immediate universe. The Demical Classification has been usually evading this notational obligation by using 9 to represent "other classes," this *i.e.*, classes other than those represented by 1 to 8. Though the Canon of Exhaustiveness is satisfied, this is virtually equivalent to failing to classify fully, *i.e.*, to provide for the isolation and enumeration of every possible class which may belong to one and the same array.

13911 Octave Notation

A contribtion of the Colon Classification is the use of what it has called 'Octave Notation.' It consists of denoting an infinite succession of co-ordinate classes by the digits.

1, 2, 3, ... 7, 8, 91, 92, 93, ... 97, 98, 991, 992, 993, ... 997, 998, 9991, ... 99 ... 91, ... 99 ... 92, ...
It will be seen that the digit 9 does not stand for any class by itself. So to speak it sacrifices its right to represent a class in its array in order to enrich infinitely the capacity of the remaining 8 digits—an emotionless analogue to what great men have said about the potency of sacrifice. In practice, the Colon Classification exploits this Octave Device even more than what is indicated above. It generalises the concept behind 'octave' and throws also the capital letters of the alphabet, which forms part of its notational armoury, into the formation of generalised octaves—thus leading to the utilisation of the last, penultimate, etc., of the octaves in an infinite sequence of octaves.

13912 International Acceptance

It is gratifying that the octave notation (though not in its generalised form) was accepted for consideration, at the Hague Conference (1948) of the International Federation for Documentation and received approval at the Ascona Conference (1950). No doubt its application to the Universal Decimal Classification will require many re-adjustments in the schedules. But work—at least thought—has been initiated along right lines.

CHAPTER 14

Field of Knowledge

There are many infinite universes of discourse which may need classification in the third sense. The one whose classification is being studied actively by the library profession is the Field of Knowledge. It will therefore be convenient to examine the experiences met with in knowledge-classification, as practised by the library profession, and to search for further qualities which class numbers should possess in order to meet the demands of an infinite universe.

141 A Universe of Classes

has been shown in the *Prolegomena* that it is convenient, and even more effective than otherwise, to regard the universe of discourse of knowledge-classification as a universe of classes—*i.e.*, to regard each specific subject, which is an existent in the field of knowledge, as a Class. This really amounts to emphasising the fact that no Unitary Class is possible in the universe of knowledge—*i.e.*, every class, however great its intension can be further subdivided.

142 Complexity of the Problem

It may here be recalled, as stated in section 122, that to classify is a neural necessity. The nervous system is an abstracting mechanism. All sensations are themselves some kind of abstraction. The cortex is the specialised part of the nervous system which carries the abstraction to more and more rarified levels and forms new combinations and permutations—

association—of the abstractions. All knowledge is some kind of abstraction at levels of different rarification, of different character and of varying precision and intensity. Formation of classes is a form of abstraction involved in the building of knowledge. Formation of classes of individuals, as even a child does, is an abstraction at a level which is already rarified. But formation of classes is an abstraction at a level of still greater rarification and this is what is involved in the classification of the Field of Knowledge. This is therefore in more urgent need of formalisation than classification of individuals. The classification of every infinite universe will need this formalisation.

143 Act of Classifying

The act of classifying a piece of embodied or expressed knowledge usually involves three stages :—

Stage 1 : Determining the specific subject embodied or expressed ;

Stage 2 : Finding from the schedule of classes that class which is co-extensive with the specific subject determined ; and

Stage 3 : Picking out from the schedule the class number given against the class so found and using it to represent the specific subject determined. This is really equivalent to translating the name of the specific subject into the preferred classificatory language.

144 Occasions of Misfit

Since the field of knowledge is infinite, occasions will often arise when there is no class in the schedule of classification which fits co-extensively with the specific subject determined. This may be due to one of two causes:

(1) The scheme of classification in use may have failed to list it though it was either known or anticipated; or

(2) The specific subject may be a new formation in the field of knowledge, which could have been neither known nor even anticipated previously.

In the circumstance, there are three possible courses: (1) to choose a loose-fitting or more extensive class number to represent it; or (2) to give it a new class number violating helpful order, because no class number can be inserted at the most helpful place needed; or (3) to give it a new class number which fits it exactly and also gives it a helpful place among the already existing or enumerated classes. What could be done on such occasions will depend upon the nature of the classification in use. This will be considered in chapters 15 to 17.

145 New Formations in the Field of Knowledge

In the meantime it will be convenient to examine the different ways in which new specific subjects are thrown forth by the field of knowledge. We shall call them the 'Tactics of the Field of Knowledge'. The notational device, by which the demands of the field of knowledge are met, may be called 'Counter-Tactics'. The tactics of the field of knowledge have been more fully described in the two papers *Library classification and international documentation* (1948) published in the *Review of documentation* of the F. I. D. and the *Self-perpetuating classification* (1949) published in the *Journal of documentation* of the ASLIB. Here is a summary:

Name and Description of Tactics	Notational Counter-Tactics.
1 Dissections :—Forming co-ordinate classes—Array of classes.	Octave notation, Chronological Device and Subject Device.
2 Denudation :—Forming sub-ordinate classes—Chain of classes.	Decimal-fraction-notation.
3 Lamination :—Super-imposition of classes taken from different arrays in two or more facets, *i.e.*, formed on the basis of different trains of characteristics — Facet formation.	Facet-analysis—Faceted notation with connecting symbols according to facet formula.
4 Loose-Assemblage :—Linkage of two or more main classes or sub-classes thereof, each by itself representing a specific subject—Phase formation.	Phase-analysis—Phased notation with connecting symbols according to phase-formula.

146 Analogues

It may be helpful to find analogues for classification in different known disciplines or modes of thinking. Each one of them may bring out or at least suggest as worthy of investigation some of the hidden potentialities of classification in the third sense. The later chapters can be expressed more briefly and expeditiously if some of such analogues are indicated here as a preliminary step.

1461 LINGUISTICS

It has been already suggested in section 134 that we may regard a system of class numbers as a language. Two essential qualities of a classificatory language have already been stated—absence of synonyms and homonyms. This is on the side of semasiology. It has certain other qualities. A classificatory language may have only substantives, or substantives and conjunctions, or substantives, conjunctions and morphological aids like prepositions. This is a peculiarity of its morphology. It is known in linguistics that syntax may depend (1) solely on morphological forms, or aids like prepositions and conjunctions as in Sanskrit or German ; or (2) solely on position (the purely agglutinative language) ; or (3) on morphological forms or aids like prepositions and conjunctions as well as position in varying degrees as it happens in different natural languages. The syntax of a classificatory language depends on position and conjunctions. A bilingual dictionary may be of different kinds. It may list, in tabular form, equivalent.

(1) words, (2) phrases, (3) idioms, (4) sentences, or even a set of connected sentences.

Of course, this may look like a forced extension of the idea 'dictionary'. But it is an understandable extension. All these varieties of dictionaries are possible in a classificatory language.

1462 CARTOGRAPHY

A scheme of classification can be regarded as a map of the territory of knowledge. The usefulness of a map depends upon many factors. The least it should do is to represent all adjacent areas of the territory as adjacent in the map. This is equivalent to satisfying the Canon of Helpful Order. Its use will be increased if it can show mountains and valleys, heights and depths—if it can show the degrees of intension of the classes. This is equivalent to satisfying the Canon of Relativity. An even more helpful map is one which shows the communications that can be established between far-lying regions. This is equivalent to disclosing phase-relation. Another desirable quality is that it should be designed in such a way that additional information can be featured on it as and when the exploration of the territory proceeds, the boundaries are re-drawn and unsuspected new terrain or valley is discovered. This featuring should not involve necessity to erase and re-do what has already been shown in the map. The qualities already mentioned should persist in the enriched map also. This, it is believed, will be achieved if the Canon of Mnemonics, especially Unscheduled Mnemonics, is satisfied.

1463 TRANSFORMATION

Cartography suggests that classification can be regarded as a transformation—using this term in the mathematical sense. A transformation maps out, as it were, one space, say A, over another space, say B—using space in the abstract sense of the General Theory of Sets of Pure Mathematics. Our familiar maps are examples of transformation. Here A is the two-dimensional curved space, which is the surface of the earth—ellipsoidal surface of a diameter of about 6,000 miles—and B is the two-dimensional plane space which is a sheet of paper, say 2' by 3', or if it is a hand atlas 10" by 14". Students of cartography know that there are several ways of mapping. We can map for example so that areas are invariant, or so that shapes are invariant. It is also known that we cannot make both of them invariant. The choice of transformation is determined by the purpose of the map. We have to choose the one or the other. We cannot serve two masters at the same time, as the saying goes.

14631 Invariants in Translation

Rendering a piece of poetry into prose is also a transformation. The space called ' poetry ' is mapped on the space called 'prose'. In this transformation we seek to keep the sense invariant and change the order of words and some of the words themselves. Similarly translation from Sanskrit to English is a transformation, *i.e.*, mapping of one space over another. Here there are two ways of mapping. One way will keep the sense as a whole invariant and another can keep the sense of each word invariant. The first will have to sacrifice and change the sense of individual words taken in isolation, while the latter is often said to ' murder ' the sense as a whole. The use of the explosive word ' murder ' shows that for most purposes we want the general sense to be kept invariant in the process of mapping one language-space over another language-space.

14632 Invariants in Classification

So it is in classification. The transformation involved in classification is even more drastic than map-projection. For, in the latter the dimensions are virtually kept invariant, except in relief maps. But in the classification of the field of knowledge even the number of dimensions is changed. The field of knowledge is multi-dimensional. But a system of class numbers, of which it is a map or transformation, is uni-dimensional and in fact even more restricted ; it is also uni-directional. There can be many schemes of classification each one of which may keep some property—only one property simple or complex—invariant. When we transform the field of knowledge into a system of class numbers each specific subject in the former, whatever be its extension, corresponds to a class number in the latter. In mathematical terminology, each multi-dimensional cell in the field of knowledge corresponds to a linear interval in the field of class numbers. Adjacent cells in the field of knowledge correspond to adjacent intervals in the field of class numbers, in most cases. Cells within cells or nests of cells correspond to intervals within intervals or nests of intervals. Interpenetrating or overlapping cells get transformed in such a way that the overlapping portions appear as overlapping ones, but get torn away from all but one of the intervals of which they were overlapping portions.

Also any connection between non-adjacent cells leads to a corresponding connection in the intervals in classification. Of course, it may be stated here that the need for transferring the multi-dimensional field of knowledge into a uni-directional, uni-dimensional field of classification arose out of the need for arranging the physical entities called books into which cells in the field of knowledge get embodied. At the present stage of human evolution, man is more at home with linear space than with multi-dimensional space. He prefers arranging books linearly. This preference of ' linearness ' persists also to some extent —though not to an equal extent—in the very process of his thinking. That is why one who is an adept in classification thinks more systematically, penetratingly and exhaustively than one who is a poor classifier. Thinking, in the present stage of evolution of man, is largely conditioned by the capacity for helpful classification. Is it that he will continue like this so long as he is space-time-conscious and space-time-bound ?

14633 Expressive vs. Extensional Representation

The classification viewed as a language or a map or a transformation should reproduce the structure inherent in the field of knowledge. It should do so not only in its grosser features but even in its minutest details. For example, a class number which represents any tiny bit of the field of knowledge should have in its own make-up the structural peculiarities which characterise that bit. The extent of usefulness of a language, a map, or a transformation or a classification depends on the similarity of the structure between the empirical world of knowledge on the one hand, and the language or map or transformation or classification on the other.

When a classification is viewed as a language, this would amount to saying that the class number, (= sentence or idiom or phrase or word as the case may be) should be expressive. Connotative terms and class numbers are preferable to denotative ones. ' Cow belonging to so and so ' or ' Cow with such and such features' is preferable to ' Cow Tara'. The latter is only extensional. The former is expressive. ' The animal which is most sought and husbanded for the milk it gives for use as human food ' is preferable to ' Cow'. The former is more expressive than the latter, though neither is merely extensional as ' Tara '.

14634 Parsimonious Representatior

It may be further added that class number should be parsimonious in its make-up without sacrificing expressiveness—that is, its correct connotation should be reached with the least number of qualities with which the purpose for which it is coined can be served. For example, we should not replace the above term for ' cow ' in animal husbandry by "a vertebrate mammal with four legs . . ." This is a demand of the Law of Parsimony.

14635 Revealing Representation

The map or classification gains in usefulness if it can even reveal, *i.e.*, bring out what was missed in the original. This is the ultimate height to which the expressiveness of class number can rise.

1464 BOOLEAN ALGEBRA

Some features of classification find some slight analogies in Boolean Algebra. The relation between a universe and the array of its classes of first order corresponds to the logical sum of sets. A chain of classes corresponds to a nest. A faceted class corresponds to the logical product of sets. From the point of view of the arrangement of the classes effected, nest-formation as well as multiplication is non-commutative. That is, the order of the resulting composite classes is changed by changing the order of the constituent classes in a chain or of the facets in a facet-formula. The physical interpretation of any configuration will depend upon the factors occurring in the physical significance of the undefinables and the operators with which we start. This analogy has not yet been examined much. Its investigation may lead to many profound and rich results with which the foundation of a classificatory language can be made more lasting.

1465 STATECRAFT

The ancient book of Indian tales, *Panchatantra*, presents, another analogy suggested by the terms ' Tactics ' and 'Counter-tactics' used to describe the various modes in which new formations are hurled on us by the field of knowledge. This analogue has been the chief guiding principle in the presentation of the genesis of classification, given in the *Fundamentals*.

The most important of the five principles of statecraft—divide and rule—comes up for use more often than others. This analogue again emphasises that there can be no resting on oars for one who has to carry the craft of State down the current of time negotiating successfully all the cultural tides, social storms and alien attacks—for one who seeks to maintain orderliness in the current of thought as it swells by the downpour of ideas, confluence of constituent ideas and the gush of depth-ideas. A crowned head, it has been said, can have no rest. Classification too can have no rest. Putting the stranger or the suspect on the rack, making him confess and eliciting from him all that is necessary and sufficient to size him up, have their analogues in Phase-Analysis, Facet-Analysis, and Sharpening of Foci to the point of co-extensiveness. The Phase-Formula, Facet-Formula and Mnemonics, scheduled and unscheduled, constitute the analogue of the rack.

1466 OTHER ANALOGIES

14661 Medicine

Other analogies also have been drawn to bring out the difference between different types of classification. Medicine provides one such analogy. It may be possible to practise medicine by prescribing only patent medicines which have been made up and bottled in advance to cure certain specific diseases or groups of diseases. When variants of a specific disease appear, it is one and the same patent medicine that has to be prescribed for all of them. New diseases for which there is no patent medicine have to go without a medicine or with a wrong one. It is the latter that happens in schemes of classification which enumerate all the known specific subjects and give ready-made class numbers for them.

There is another way of practising medicine. After diagnosing the disease in all its details a prescription may be written out to suit its 'individuating particularities,' mentioning all the drugs which should be put in and the exact proportion in which they should be mixed. The pharmacy will then be asked to prepare the medicine according to the prescription.

Here there need not be any patent medicine in stock. The medicine has to be prepared in each case on demand. This is what happens in schemes of classification which do not give ready-made class numbers. Of course it is possible for an intelligent apothecary with experience to know the kind of diseases which are commonly prevalent in his area and anticipate the mixtures which are frequently in demand. He will then be wise and save considerable time by making these mixtures in bulk. Probably he will do so. In the same manner even a scheme of classification which need not give ready-made class numbers may for convenience put up a schedule of ready-made class numbers for specific subjects which commonly recur in particular types of libraries. The Colon Classification which follows the apothecary analogy has been featured as if it were an enumerative classification in *School and College libraries* (1942), and *Library organization* (1947) to suit the needs of the class of library specified in the books. It will be found similarly featured in the *Library manual* of (1951).

14662 Toy-Shop

A toy-shop provides another analogy. Ordinarily, it has toys of various kinds—all of them ready-made. Naturally the variety of toys is limited. If a child is bored with these limited varieties the shopkeeper has to lose a customer. This is what happens in the case of classification schemes which give ready-made class numbers. On the other hand the toy-shop may provide a Meccano set which contains perforated strips, bolts, nuts, wheels, strings, and so on in a suitable variety of standard sizes and shapes, with which any kind of toy can be made at will to please the varying fancies of the child. And yet, it may also have on show and for sale some particular toys built out of the very same Meccano pieces. This is what happens in a scheme like the Colon Classification which does not normally provide ready-made class numbers, though it may give illustrative schedules of ready-made class numbers.

147 Terminology of Colon Classification
Optical Analogy

In the design of its classificatory terminology, the Colon Classification has followed the optical analogue. It speaks of a number as a Focus. It refers to Sharpening of Focus. It calls a close-fitting or co-extensive class number the Sharpest Focus. It calls the specific subject itself a subject Focus. Indeed, it applies the term Focus to the expression in the classificatory as well as the natural languages. It speaks of simple, compound, and complex, and basic and dependent foci. The use of this terminology and some of the points mentioned in some of the sections of chapter 3 are perhaps better illustrated by a concrete example.

Consider the specific subject (subject focus) :—

Statistical study, in India in 1950, of the Homeopathic treatment of the tuberculosis of bones (1)

For definiteness, we shall re-arrange the words in the name of the above specific subject in the order in which their translations will appear in the classificatory language or class number, constructed according to Colon Classification. We shall also fill up the ellipses occurring in the name of the specific subject to make the translation into the class number easy.

Further, we shall insert the appropriate connecting symbols prescribed in section 1371. We get the following result :—

(Medicine) (Homeopathic) (Bones) : (Tuberculosis) : (Treatment) : (Statistical study). (India). (1950's). (2)

The translation of the above in the Colon Language is : LL81 : 421 : 6 : B28.44.N5. (3)

The following statement shows the names of the facets and the basic classes (basic foci) involved in the statements (2) and (3) mentioned above :—

(Homeopathy) (Organ) : (Problem) : (Handling) : (Statistical study). (Geography). (Chronology). (4)

Stated in terms of Fundamental Categories, (4) will be as follows :—

(Basic Personality) (Personality) : (Energy) : (Energy) : (Basic personality). (Space). (Time). (5)

1471 COMPLEX FOCUS

The specific subject mentioned in (1) and (2) and its equivalent class number mentioned in (3) are two-phased, the phases as expressed in (2) and (3) being as follows :—

Phase 1	Phase 2
(Medicine Homeopathic) (Bones) : (Tuberculosis) : (Treatment) :	(Statistical study). (India). (1950's)
LL81 : 421 : 6	B28.44.N5.

The above specific subject and class number are said

to be Complex Foci (because they are made of phases) —to be more exact, Simply Complex Foci (because there is only one additional phase).

An over-all focus with two additional phases may be said to be a Doubly Complex Focus. If it has three additional phases, it may be said to be a Triply Complex Focus and so on.

Other descriptive names for a Complex Focus are Loosely Assembled Focus or Phased Focus.

1472 COMPOUND FOCUS

The focus mentioned under Phase 1 in section 1471 is a Compound Focus because it has at least one facet—to be more exact, Triply Compound Focus (because it has three facets). The three facets are :—

In Terms of Fundamental Categories.	In Terms of their Manifestations as Attributes to the Basic Personality.
(Basic personality) (Personality) (Energy) : (Energy).	(Medicine Homeopathic) (Organ) : (Problem) : (Handling)
(BP) (P) : (E) : (E)	(LL) (O) : (P) : (H)

Other descriptive names for a Compound Focus are Laminated Focus and Faceted Focus.

1473 BASIC FOCUS

In (7) the term 'Basic Personality' in the first column gets replaced by the term 'Medicine Homeopathic' in the second column. It is as a result of this that the facet 'Personality' in the first column manifests itself in column 2 as 'Organ Facet'. It is again due to the same reason that the first 'Energy Facet' in the first column manifests itself in the second column as 'Problem Facet'. This may be generalised in the form :—The manifestations of the Fundamental Categories are determined in accordance with the context set by the Main or Canonical Class or Subject to which they are attributes. Of course every Main or Canonical Class is itself a manifestation of Personality—Super-personality, we may say—which has the potentiality to have several facets which are manifestations of any or all of the Fundamental Categories. Since, at the level of Class Numbers, the numbers belonging to each facet can have a definite meaning, if and only if they are placed in relation to a number representing a Main or Canonical Subject, a Main or Canonical Subject as well as its equivalent Class Number is called a 'Basic Focus'.

1474 DEPENDENT FOCUS

The very factor, which calls for a Main or Canonical Class being called a Basic Focus, calls also for the focus in a facet to be called a 'Dependent Focus'. This term applies equally to its expression in the classificatory language as well as in the natural language. The epithet 'Dependent' is appropriate because it cannot represent a specific subject unless it is attached to a basic focus. Its meaning is dependent on the Basic Focus.

1475 SIMPLE FOCUS

If we have a specific subject which consists only of a Basic Focus and is not uni-focal in any of its facets other than an amplifying one we call it a 'Simple Focus'. For example, a general treatise or text-book on Homeopathy or in Medicine in general is said to have a Simple Focus. This term applies equally to its expression in the classificatory language as well as in the natural language.

Statements similar to those made in section 1472 to 1475 in relation to the first phase of the specific subject (1) can also be made in relation to its second phase. In fact,

> 'Statistical study in India in the 1950's is a Compound Focus; with statistical study as its Basic Focus.

1476 SHARPNESS OF FOCUS

We recognise three modes of sharpening a subject focus.

14761 Sharpening by Loose Assemblage (Complex Focus)

The focus of the specific subject (1) is sharper than either of the specific subjects (compound foci) mentioned in (7) and (8). Even if the complex focus is made of two simple foci, it will still be sharper than either of them. In conformity with the terminology given in section 145, we shall say that a Complex Focus is got by the Loose-assemblage of two or more foci, simple or compound. We may say that the first constituent focus is sharpened by loose assemblage.

14762 Sharpening by Lamination

The focus of the specific subject of (7) is sharper than that of the Simple Focus, Homeopathic Medicine. It can also be easily seen that the addition of each facet adds to the sharpness of the Basic Focus. In conformity with the terminology given in section 145 we shall say that a Compound Focus is got by the Lamination of one or more Dependent Foci on a Basic Focus.

14763 Sharpening by Denudation

Consider the following chain of classes in the first Energy Facet of the first phase given in (6) :

4 = Disease
↓
42 = Infectious disease
↓
421 = Tuberculosis

Each link in the above chain is made sharper and turned into the next link by decreasing the extension, which is generally reflected in the notation by the addition of another digit. In conformity with the terminology given in section 145 we shall say that a Dependent Focus—that is Focus within a Facet—is sharpened by Denudation.

14764 Basic Facet

It may be stated here that basic Personality itself can be sharpened by Denudation. This is equivalent to saying that a Simple Focus can appear in different degrees of sharpness and that the increase in sharpness is got by Denudation. This similarity between a Simple Focus and a Dependent Focus within a facet suggests that for certain purposes we may look upon a Simple Focus itself as belonging to a Facet. When we so look upon it we shall call it the 'Basic Facet'.

14765 Specific Subject

It may be repeated here that there can be no specific subject without a Basic Facet. But a focus in a Basic Facet can by itself be a specific subject. This can be put again in another form which may be of use in certain situations. A Basic Facet is always necessary and may also be sufficient to form a specific

Subject. On the other hand, a Dependent Focus is neither necessary nor sufficient to form a specific subject.

We may also make the following analogous statement: One phase is always necessary and proves sufficient to make a specific subject. Additional phases by themselves are not necessary to form a specific subject. But they may occur.

14766 Varieties of Basic Focus

It must be remembered in this connection that a Basic Focus is either a Main Class or an Amplified Main Class (as defined in the *Fundamentals*) or a Canonical Division of a Main Class (as defined in the *Colon classification*). A Main Class is what is enumerated as a Main Class in a scheme of classification

1477 DISTINCTION BETWEEN FACET AND PHASE

The above analysis suggests an answer to the question often put by those who are new to facet- and phase-analysis but not till now answered in an objective way without going beyond the rules of classification themselves. The question is, 'How to distinguish between facet and phase ?' The answer now available is, 'A phase is a simple or compound focus which contains a Basic Focus within itself'. Further it is by itself equivalent to the name of a specific subject. On the contrary, a facet can by itself present only a dependent focus. A focus in a facet cannot by itself represent a specific subject. It is only when it is compounded with a Basic Focus that a specific subject comes to be represented .

148 Potency of the Concepts in Colon Classification

Though the concrete example (in section 147),

selected to secure shortness and directness of exposition, contained the class number according to the Colon Classification, it should not be thought that the concepts brought out are peculiar only to that scheme of classification. For, the availability of the method implied in this approach to the break-down of a specific subject is not a property imposed on the field of knowledge by the Colon Classification. It is a property inherent in the field of knowledge. All that may be said is that it was the structure of the notation of the Colon Classification which first emphasised and made explicit this implicit property of the field of knowledge. Strictly speaking, it is the field of knowledge which has imposed this property of itself on 'classification in the third sense'. The Colon Classification is but a creature of this imposition. This imposition, however, is not a violence or burden on classification. On the other hand, it is a welcome help and enrichment.

1481 MECHANISATION OF FINDING HELPFUL PLACE FOR A NEW SUBJECT

For, the distinctive function of classification in the third sense is to provide an artificial language of ordinal numbers into which the names of all specific subjects—known as well as at-present-unknown formations in the field of knowledge—may be translated, so that the maintenance of the preferred, helpful arrangement of known specific subjects can be mechanised and the finding of an appropriate helpful place amidst them for new specific subjects, as and when they come to be known, may also be mechanised to a considerable extent. Yes. The notational apparatus of a classification should facilitate even this latter task in a great measure. This is what the analogy of linguistics indicated in section 1461 suggests as a desirable quality of 'classification in the third sense'.

1482 ADVANTAGES OF A STRUCTURED NOTATION

The analogy of map-projection and transformation indicated in sections 1462 and 1463 suggests the desirability of objectively determining the features that should be kept invariant during the process of 'classification in the third sense,' so that it may be most helpful for the purpose for which classification is designed. Moreover, the imposition, made by the field of knowledge on class number, makes the class number preserve and show forth some helpful feature in the structure of the specific subject itself. Since, as stated in section 122, holding on to the structural feature of ideas is a neural necessity in man, a classification, which accepts and assimilates the imposition of the field of knowledge, indicated in section 147, is able to fulfil efficiently the functions assigned to it by the Laws of Library Science, *viz*., (1) to increase the chance for recorded materials and expressed thought to get used by those who seek them and also by those who can thereby be enabled to think, feel and act more efficiently; and (2) to arrange the recorded materials and the records about them in catalogues, bibliographies and other aids to documentation service in such a way that the subjective as well as the objective time of the consumers can be conserved.

1483 AMENABILITY TO METHODS LIKE BOOLEAN ALGEBRA

This imposition of the field of knowledge on ' classification in the third sense' makes the latter amenable to be assessed, corrected and developed by methods like Boolean Algebra which ruthlessly keep out the inexorable fallacies which usually creep in unawares and vitiate thinking and acting when done through the medium of a natural language.

CHAPTER 15

Enumerative Classification

We say that a scheme of 'classification in the third sense' is 'enumerative' when applied to the field of knowledge, if it enumerated all possible specific subjects in a preferred helpful order along with their respective class numbers. As the arrangement is 'more or less helpful,' it follows that it should be according to class numbers, *i.e.*, according to the names of specific subjects in the classificatory language and not according to the arrangement implied in their names in a natural language. Field of knowledge being infinite, it is sure to throw forth from time to time new specific subjects which could not have been anticipated at all at the time the scheme of classification was designed. These new specific subjects could not be given their class numbers by the classifiers. Their classification should be held up until the classificationist finds class numbers for them. Now-a-days new specific subjects are pouring in every day even at the level of books. The classificationist therefore becomes a bottleneck and becomes the cause of considerable time-lag in the organisation of knowledge and the books embodying them.

1501 Schedule of Classification

Viewed as a dictionary, the first column of a schedule of classification gives the class numbers in their ordinal order and the second column gives their meanings in a natural language. The alphabetical index to the schedule gives the dictionary in the opposite way. The first column gives the names of specific subjects in a natural language in an alphabetical order and the second column gives their respective class numbers. The schedule in an enumerative classification turns out to be a dictionary of sentences—very much like a conversation-lexicon designed to help a foreign traveller by including the commonly recurring statements or questions. In using a conversation-lexicon there is no need for the foreign tourist to bother himself much about grammar. So it is with the classifier. He need not bother himself much with the rules of classification.

In a sense however the schedule of an enumerative classification is not selective like a tourist conversation-lexicon. To that extent it also loses in its slimness. A well-prepared schedule of classification attempts to provide class numbers for all specific subjects which are either known to exist or can be anticipated to appear. This exhaustiveness is however only apparent. Just as the tourist will not find his conversation-lexicon to be of any use when he has to express ideas not provided for in the lexicon, the classifier too will not be able to classify new specific subjects not provided in the schedule.

151 Congress Classification

Among the well-known printed schemes of classification, the Congress Classification is the nearest approximation to a pure enumerative classification. It is not quite pure since it gives as tables appended to the enumerative part certain schedules of attachments which the classifier can use as and when a new specific subject calling for its use arises. The words used in the description of such a table are significant.

They are, " For the uniform arrangement of general material in all schedules". To enable the classifier to make a correct and intelligible combination between a class number in the main schedule and an attachment given in the appended tables, some rules of grammar have to be provided by the scheme. But these tables come in for use very occasionally so that the Congress Classification is predominantly enumerative.

Generally speaking the specific subjects are enumerated in a 'more or less helpful ' order. There are however regions where unhelpful alphabetical arrangement is preferred to any sort of possible helpful classified order. The schedules of authors in literature is an example. A usual explanation for this deviation from helpful order is that shelf-arrangement is easier that way and that Congress Classification is essentially a scheme dictated by the exigencies of shelf arrangement in the Library of Congress. This cannot be the real reason. For the needs of shelf-arrangement alone will justify all books being arranged by the alphabet in the name of the authors or at least all specific subjects by the alphabets in their names—analogous to the subject entries in an alphabetico-classed or dictionary catalogue. The real unexpressed reason for this regression to unhelpful (from the point of view of the Laws of Library Science and the predominantly subject approach of readers) alphabetical arrangement, appears to be the incapacity of the integer-notation adopted, to provide for infinite interpolations between any two consecutive class numbers.

1511 ANALOGY WITH LINGUISTICS

The potential vocabulary of the Congress Classification is restricted. Indeed it is finite. It is limited by the sizes of the gaps left between consecutive class numbers already ear-marked in the schedule for definite specific subjects. When the number of new specific subjects claiming their helpful places within one gap exceeds the capacity of that gap, they cannot all be individualised. They cannot be given distinctive class numbers. The situation will be like asking two or more guests to share the same chair when they are greater in number than the number of chairs available. Some of the new specific subjects cannot be given closely fitting, co-extensive class numbers. This is because the design of the Congress Language is not based on the enumeration of the ultimates like phonemes, radicals, variants derived by morphological or syntactical means, etc., from out of which words and sentences can be constructed to express any idea. It is like the primitive language which contains only explosive expressions or radicals which yield nothing intelligible when analysed and broken down into parts or ultimates.

On account of these features, classificatory experience confined to Congress Classification may even lead one to deny that a classification scheme is an artificial language of ordinal numbers.

1512 ANALOGY WITH CARTOGRAPHY

Even specific subjects, which appear when there are still vacancies left in the gap appropriate to their helpful placing, cannot be thrown into helpful order in the Congress Classification, as they will not put in their appearance exactly in the order which their helpful arrangement would demand. This means that, viewed as a map, whereas we have a good map so far as the basic schedule is concerned, it fails to provide the means for representing adjacent areas of the original as adjacent areas in the map, when minuter or new areas are explored long after the original map was drawn. In other words, all new specific subjects do not fall into a ' more or less helpful ' order. This fault is further intensified by the fact that the gap between two consecutive class numbers already used has to provide hospitality in array as well as hospitality in chain. The methodology of Congress Classification does not provide any means of distinguishing between these two types of hospitality. The result is that co-ordinate classes and subordinate classes are promiscuously thrown together. When the gaps are filled in this way, chaos sets in and the very negation of classification happens. In other words, Congress Classification is a true map of the field of knowledge only in so far as the details of the field were known at the time the map was drawn. But it becomes thoroughly untrustworthy and unhelpful in so far as the details, discovered later, are put on it.

1513 ANALOGY WITH TRANSFORMATION

All these can also be put in the language of transformation. Cells in the multidimensional space in the field of knowledge are not infrequently transformed by the Congress Classification into intervals in the one-directional one-dimensional space of class numbers, which are either without any analogue to the orientation of the original cell or are truly points without any length whatever, *i.e.*, either the entire contents of a cell are compressed into a single point—very much like certain projective transformations which compress the entire extent of the region usually known as infinity into a 'point at infinity'—or the cell is crushed into several points which lose their original moorings and attachment and settle down in an interval of the one-dimensional space, in some random order. In other words, the transformation effected by the Congress Classification fails to keep invariant the connectedness of minuter regions.

1514 ANALOGY WITH BOOLEAN ALGEBRA

The failure of the Congress Classification in regard to new formations in the field of knowledge may perhaps be given an analogy in Boolean Algebra. Let us call the field of knowledge the total space of the algebra and the specific subjects as sub-spaces contained in it. The algebra of some of the sub-spaces which are very minute, indeed which have been too-minute to have been sensed at the beginning, is different from the algebra of the total space. There is something tricky about this. It needs finding out if Boolean algebras worked out so far can be applied to such a universe. Even if they can be, there is no doubt that they will be more complicated than those suited to spaces where the same system of algebra can be applied to a sub-space of any order whatever. If classification can be designed to suit a more simple type of Boolean algebra, surely that would be preferable.

1515 ANALOGY WITH STATECRAFT

To draw from the analogy of statecraft, the notation of the Congress Classification has only a limited stock of counter-tactics. It soon gets outwitted by the superior tactics of the field of knowledge. It soon gets rigid. It soon gets frozen. It soon loses all nimbleness. It is unable to face the subtleties in the tactics of the enemy to be subdued—the field of knowledge.

The discomfiture, helplessness and defeat of the Congress Classification when faced by minute specific or micro-units of thought newly thrown against it, are best pictured in an exquisite episode in the *Ramayana*, the premier epic poem of India. Hanuman, the messenger of the hero Rama, is flying across from the main land of India to the neighbouring island of Ceylon. An old witch appears and claims him as a prey on the ground that law allows her to capture and devour anybody who flies across that region. Hanuman says, "You need not take the trouble to seize me. I shall myself enter your mouth if only you open it big enough for my body". She gapes open her mouth. Hanuman becomes bigger. She makes her mouth wider still. Hanuman makes his body a little bigger. The race goes on between them. When the witch had opened her mouth to the point of her vocal muscle becoming too stiff for the jaws to be easily moved, with extraordinary agility Hanuman makes his body extremely tiny and flies through her mouth. The witch accepts defeat and suddenly remembers this happening as the signal mentioned at the time she was cursed to become a witch. The dawn of this memory retransforms her into her original, pleasant, non-witch-self; for the curse leaves her.

1516 Other Analogies

To use the analogy of medicine, the Congress Classification is like a chest of patent medicine. It is convenient to use and very effective for a limited number of diseases. It is of no use or at least not sufficiently effective when new diseases appear.

To use the analogy of toy-shop, Congress Classification is like a shop of finished toys. It cannot produce new toys to suit the fancy of all children.

1517 Optical Analogy and Terminology

Broadly speaking, the Congress notation is structureless. It does not disclose the fundamental constituent concepts out of which a specific subject is formed as a derived composite concept. The result is that from the form of the Congress number we cannot infer anything whatever about the extension or the intension of the specific subject it represents. The length of the Congress number does not conform to the Canon of Relativity. Practically all the Congress numbers have virtually the same length. This failure of utilising variation in the number of digits to serve some classificatory purpose amounts to a huge wastage of one of the resources of classificatory technique. This wastage leads indeed to the chagrin of the Law of Parsimony and its legitimate protest.

The specific subjects enumerated in the Congress Classification and the order in which they are enumerated together lend themselves to be described with profit in terms of the optical terminology set forth in section 147. At the idea-level, we have Basic Foci, Simple Foci, Dependent Foci, Compound Foci of different orders, Complex Foci of different orders, Facets, Phases and the Sharpening of Foci at different levels. But all this richness is hidden away at the notation-level by the dull, uniform, structureless class numbers of the Congress Classification.

1518 LOSS OF POTENCY

The limitations which the otherwise excellent Congress Classification brings upon itself by not making the optical terminology as applicable to its class numbers as to the analysis and naming of the specific subjects themselves, will be seen in chapter 17. Its primitive notation takes away from its potency considerably.

152 Decimal Classification

Among the well-known printed schemes of classication, the Decimal Classification should also be counted as a predominantly enumerative classification. Its approximation to a pure enumerative classification is not as near as that of the Congress Classification. For, the viability of its class numbers is of a higher order. Its Common Subdivisions, Table of Languages and Philological Tables are far more general than the tables appended to any volume of the Congress Classification. Apart from these—explicitly called auxiliary—tables, the geographical schedules built as part of the main structure of the Decimal Classification is also frequently used as an auxiliary table. The non-enumerative element of the Decimal Classification is even more widespread. For its main tables are studded here and there with rules like "Divided as the whole classification", "Divided like the class 600," etc. In spite of these deviations, the Decimal Classification is predominantly enumerative.

Generally speaking, the specific subjects are enumerated in a 'more or less helpful' order. It seldom prescribes unhelpful alphabetical arrangement, even to the point of our wondering whether it eschews alphabetical arrangement even where it can be used with profit. It avoids alphabetical arrangement in spite of its declaring that it is designed primarily for shelf-arrangement without undue dominance by considerations of logic or relationship.

1521 ANALOGY OF LINGUISTICS

The potential vocabulary of the Decimal Classification is also restricted though not as much as the Congress Classification. It is no doubt infinite and yet not as infinite—if such an expression can be used—as the number of specific subjects which the field of knowledge has the potentiality to throw forth. The order of infinity of its potential vocabulary is that of its decimal-fraction-notation. A concrete example will illustrate the way in which the Decimal Vocabulary stands restricted. The following items are taken from the Decimal Dictionary:—

378 Secondary education

375 Curriculum

But the dictionary gives no Decimal Number for 'Curriculum in secondary education.' The classifier is therefore obliged to club it forcibly either with secondary education or with curriculum. He has also to take special care to see that he is consistent in this forced clubbing. The situation is like having only two chairs in a room, each of which is occupied. When a third person appears he has to sit on the lap of one of these two. This is similar to what happens in Congress Classification. Consistency from library to library is impracticable. Merril's *Code for classifiers* has demonstrated this. Some of the new specific subjects cannot be given closely fitting co-extensive class numbers. Classificatory experience confined to Decimal Classification may therefore even lead one to deny that a classification scheme is an artificial language of ordinal numbers.

1522 ANALOGY OF CARTOGRAPHY

Generally speaking the Decimal Classification provides a good map of the field of knowledge so far as the basic schedule is concerned and even in relation to certain classes of minuter areas which may be newly discovered. But it cannot accommodate all such minuter areas. The fault of the Congress Classification which disables it from distinguishing Hospitality in Chain and Hospitality in Array is not however inherent in the methodology of the Decimal Classification. Co-ordinate classes and subordinate classes can always be kept apart as and when new specific subjects appear. However, the methodology for doing this correctly is not explicitly stated in its rules. It therefore happens that classifiers who have more notational freedom to form new class numbers in the Decimal Classification than in the Congress Classification, often use the same decimal-fraction-device to provide either type of hospitality and cause unhelpfulness in arrangement. With some care and training in the fundamental principles of classification, classifiers can be educated to avoid this error. The education needed is to make them sensitive enough to distinguish between the cases where the Octave Notation should be used and those in which Decimal-Fraction-Notation should be used.

1523 ANALOGY WITH TRANSFORMATION

Cells in the multi-dimensional space in the field of knowledge are easily transformed by the Decimal Classification into intervals in the one-directional, one-dimensional space of class numbers, with a few exceptions. A compound cell which is a cluster of sub-cells in the multi-dimensional space of the field of knowledge is transformed into a complex interval which is a cluster of sub-intervals in the linear space of class numbers. The fault in the Decimal transformation is that the sub-cell which is transformed into the end sub-interval is fully represented in the linear space of class numbers. But all the other sub-cells are liable to be wrongly transformed. Some of them may be altogether omitted and some may be transformed into the same sub-interval as some other sub-cells along with which it forms a nest of sub-cells.

1524 ANALOGY WITH BOOLEAN ALGEBRA

The failure of the Decimal Classification in regard to a cluster of sub-cells in the field of knowledge can be explained in terms of Boolean Algebra by saying that the field of Decimal numbers does not always contain products of two numbers. In certain sub-fields like 63 Education, the products are totally absent. In certain sub-fields like 61 Medicine there is inconsistency. For, products exist in some cases and do not exist in other cases. This inconsistency is bewildering to beginners, if Decimal Classification is taught and used along rational lines. But if it is taught in the spirit of 'have it or leave it' without taking the learner into confidence or if it is used in the spirit of "hit or miss" without investigating the reasons behind it, the bewilderingness of the Decimal Classification may not be seen.

1525 ANALOGY WITH STATECRAFT

To draw from the analogy of statecraft, the notation of the Decimal Classification is more resourceful in its counter-tactics than that of the Congress Classification. But by no means it is sufficient. It too soon gets outwitted by the superior tactics of the field of knowledge. Its exterior is resilient, fluid and nimble. But its inside is rigid, frozen and without any nimbleness. This elastic veneer covering what is rigid inside is dangerous. It misleads persons to belief that it is everywhere elastic. In fact textbooks on classification indiscriminately describe the Decimal Notation as a whole to be elastic when the fact is that it is only its tip that is elastic. The field of knowledge is too resourceful to be misled by the elastic appearance of the tip and to take defeat. On the other hand its tactics is to attack the Decimal Number anywhere other than the tip. The decimal notation stands overpowered since it knows of no counter-tactics to meet such a manoeuvre of the field of knowledge. The discomfiture, helplessness and defeat of the Decimal Classification become manifest when it has to face the minute specific subjects or micro-units of thought being thrown forth now-a-days by the field of knowledge. In the era in which the Decimal Classification was designed, the problem of micro-units of thought had not arisen. The majority of the materials which challenged the organisation at that time were books that embodied only micro-units of thought. Monographs, reprints of articles and pamphlets had not then become as plentiful as they are today. The new generation of librarians must develop a new attitude unhampered by the limited resources of the Decimal Notation which were fairly adequate in the past to meet the limited tactics of the micro-units of thought thrown forth by the field of knowledge.

1526 OTHER ANALOGIES

To use the analogy of Medicine, the Decimal Classification is like a chest of patent medicine with a few bottles of chemicals in bulk. When new diseases which differ from the old diseases only to a limited extent, it is possible in some cases to make the patent medicine more effective by the addition of a few drops from the appropriate bottle of chemicals. But even this will prove to be of no use or at least to be not sufficiently effective when altogether new diseases appear.

To use the analogy of toy-shop, Decimal Classification is like a shop of finished toys with just a few extra attachments which can be added on in some cases to produce slightly different toys. But it cannot produce totally new toys to suit the fancy of all children

1527 OPTICAL ANALOGY AND TERMINOLOGY

Really speaking, the Decimal Notation is structureless. The purity of its notation which recognises no digit other than Arabic numerals fails to disclose that a specific subject is formed as a derived composite concept by a combination of fundamental constituent concepts. It must be repeated here as an aside that the decimal point in the Decimal Notation has no substantive function. It is not at all significant. It is said to be inserted to give relief to the eye or to the breath in reading out the number. But this cannot be consistently maintained as there are Decimal Numbers which pile up a dozen digits after the decimal point without any other decimal point to separate them. But the Decimal Notation conforms to the Canon of Relativity. It is possible to separate the digits in a Decimal Number according to the different facets to which they belong. Indeed it has been long my practice as a teacher and as an examiner to set the breaking up of Decimal Numbers into facets and the naming of them, as an exercise. The Congress Numbers are no doubt beyond redemption in this matter. But it is most tantalising that the Decimal Numbers which do have facets in them hide them away. Indeed they have been hiding them so thoroughly that it took several years to recognise and refer to them explicitly. Even now there are classifiers who say that it is something read into the Decimal Classification which has nothing of this sort in its intrinsic make-up.

The specific subjects enumerated in the Decimal Classification and the order in which they are enumerated together respect and lend themselves so far as they go, to be described with profit in terms of the optical terminology set forth in section 147. We have

Basic Foci, Simple Foci, Dependent Foci and Compound Foci of different orders. We have also Facets, and occasionally even Phases but very often the Facets and the Phases are not distinguishable. The sharpening of Foci is not possible at all levels. In this respect the enumeration of specific subjects is not as rich in the Decimal Classification as in the Congress Classification. But whatever richness it possesses is hidden away by its structureless, inexpressive, class numbers.

1528 LOSS OF POTENCY

The decimal-fraction-notation has no doubt increased the potency of the Decimal Classification to a higher level than that of the Congress Classification. The separate schedules for Common Subdivisions and the free and conscious use of the Subject Device, though not so named, also adds to its potency. But the failure to exploit fully the Octave Notation, and to provide a distinct connecting symbol, with a defined ordinal value, to show transition from one facet to another and thereby exploit the faceted-notation to its fullest extent, has not only depleted its potency but also failed to provoke further thought in the discipline of classification. This latter responsibility attaches itself to the Decimal Classification because it was the pioneer 'classification in the third sense' that opened up new trails and captured the imagination of thousands of librarians in the world.

CHAPTER 16

Analytico-Synthetic Classification

We say that a scheme of 'classification in the third sense', is 'analytico-synthetic' when applied to the field of knowledge, if it does not enumerate specific subjects which are derived composite concepts but gives only schedules of fundamental constituent concepts with their respective numbers. We do not therefore have a single schedule as in enumerative classification. What we do have is a series of schedules in which the fundamental constituent concepts are arranged in a 'more or less helpful' order and therefore according to their numbers, *i.e.*, according to the names of the specific concepts in the classificatory language but not according to the arrangement implied in their names in a natural language. Some of this series of schedules are ubiquitous. That is, they are likely to be drawn from in constructing class number belonging to several regions of the field of knowledge. The majority of the rest of the series of schedules fall into groups. Each group of schedules is applicable only to stated subjects, usually referred to as Main Classes and Canonical Classes. This avoidance of listing specific subjects gives an analytico-synthetic classification the capacity to put up a distinctive class number to denote any specific subject that may be thrown forth by the field of knowledge in the future in addition to those that have been thrown forth in the past or present. But this advantage is got at what may appear to be a disadvantage to the classifiers, for, hardly any specific subject other than a Main Class or a Canonical Class will have its class number stated in the scheme. It will have to be constructed by (1) first breaking down the specific subject into its fundamental constituent concepts ; (2) picking out from the appropriate schedules enumerated in the scheme the corrected number for each of these concepts ; and (3) synthesising the numbers so picked out, in a prescribed way. When described in words, this may look like a very complicated process. On the other hand it will be shown in chapter 17 that this procedure helps a classifier much more than the hide and seek which he has to play amidst the enormous number of pages of an enumerative classification. It is found from experience that the extent of 'hide and seek' in an analytico-synthetic classification is confined largely to two or three pages in the hunt for each constituent number. Experience of students, who have learnt both an enumerative and an analytico-synthetic classification with equal emphasis and thought, also shows that a beginner soon learns that it is more comfortable to work with an analytico-synthetic classification than with an enumerative one. This is what many of my students have reported to me. There has been ample evidence of the same reaction in the examinees in three universities where the two types of classification are taught and are made to figure in the examination papers on a co-ordinate and comparative basis.

1601 SCHEDULE OF CLASSIFICATION

Viewed as a dictionary, the schedule part of an analytico-synthetic classification is like a dictionary of words and phrases and not at all like a conversation-lexicon referred to in section 1501. It is more like an ordinary bilingual dictionary which helps us to pass on from a word or phrase in the classificatory language to its equivalent in a natural language. The alphabetical index which is to serve in the opposite way has necessarily to be more complicated. Even in a well-prepared alphabetical index of an enumerative classification, the index has to be somewhat complicated in appearance. Indeed one of the contributions of the *Decimal classification* is the 'Relative index' which is apparently complicated but really helpful. The complication reaches even a higher level, in its appearance, in the alphabetical index of an analytico-synthetic classification. But it is much more compact. The index part to the *Colon classification* illustrates this. There is one other remark which experience dictates. The schedule-part of an analytico-synthetic classification is extremely thin. Not even a hundredth part of a fully enumerative classification like the Congress Classification and not even a tenth part of an enumerative classification studded with synthetic elements, like the Decimal Classification. In addition to this the automatic reduction of the number of pages to be searched at a time for a single fundamental constituent concept to two or three, as stated already, reduces the number of occasions for referring to the majority of the entries in alphabetical index to a negligibly small one. The alphabetical index relates only to the dependant foci in the several facets.

1600 RULES OF CLASSIFICATION

It is well known that the capacity to use a dictionary is, though necessary, not sufficient to translate from one language to another. This is because dictionaries give only translations of words and phrases and never of passages-- sentences or paragraphs. So it is when we have to translate the name of a specific subject in a natural language into an analytico-synthetic classificatory language. For, as it is already stated, the schedule of classification is in this case very much like a dictionary which connects only the words in two natural languages. The additional qualification needed in translation is (1) a knowledge of the grammar of both the languages and particularly of the foreign one, and (2) capacity to re-arrange the ideas and therefore the words of the first language, as a preliminary measure, in an order which is in accord with the genius of the second language. All this amounts to saying that a classifier should know the rules of classification prescribed for use in connection with an analytico-synthetic classification.

161 Colon Classification

Among the well-known printed schemes of classification the Colon Classification is perhaps the first of the analytico-synthetic variety. It is a pure example of that variety. Its preliminary schedules include those of (1) Main Classes, (2) Common Subdivisions, (3) Geographical Divisions, (4) Language Divisions, and (5) Chronological Divisions. Then follow one chapter for each of the Main Classes. In each chapter, if the Main Class is not broken down in the first instance into Canonical Divisions, there are usually one or two schedules corresponding to the one or two trains of characteristics which are relevant to its classification. In other words, the facets of the Main Class are mentioned and the foci in each of them are enumerated. If the Main Class is broken down into Canonical Divisions in the first instance, such of the Canonical Divisions as admit of them are provided with similar schedules based on the trains of characteristics relevant to their classification. Generally speaking the divisions in each of the above-mentioned schedules are enumerated in a 'more or less helpful' order. There are however regions where alphabetical arrangement is prescribed in the form 'Divide by Alphabetical Device'; and there are definite rules which prescribe the minimum arrangement is prescribed in the form number of the initial letters which should be used to secure individualisation. An example of this will be found in the Full Crop Schedule worked out for Agriculture in the *Abgila* of March 1950. It will be found that the international name of crops is prescribed to be used for Alphabetical Device. The Alphabetical Device is used only when there is strong evidence to show that there is no other arrangement which is at all helpful. The point is that when none of the possible arrangements has more of the element of helpfulness than the purely alphabetical one, the alphabetical arrangement scores because people are more familiar with it.

1610 RULES OF CLASSIFICATION

The first part of *Colon classification* is entitled 'Rules of classification'. It gives objective definition of Class

Number and of most other concepts. In the preliminary chapters it describes various devices by which class numbers should be constructed. What are called Facet- and Phase-Formulae are defined. These formulae enable one to analyse a given specific subject in a systematic manner and rearrange the words in the name of the specific subject filling up ellipses if any, as a preliminary to the construction of the class number. The facet-formula of the main class or canonical division to which the specific subject belongs helps in this analysis and break-down of the specific subject into its fundamental constituent elements. Connecting symbols are prescribed by the rules and also indicated in the facet-and phase-formulae for synthesising the fundamental constituent numbers, got by translating the fundamental constituent concept, into the derived composite class number as the translation of the name of the specific subject. It is this process of first analysing the specific subject and at the last stage synthesising the class number which makes the Colon Classification an analytico-synthetic classification.

1611 ANALOGY WITH LINGUISTICS

The potential vocabulary of the Colon Classification is infinite. Its infinity is of a higher order than that of the Decimal Classification. The order of infinity of its potential vocabulary is that of the number of facets and phases its notation can accommodate. To take the example given in section 1521, we saw that it is impossible to get a Decimal Number for the specific subject 'Curriculum in secondary education'. But we can provide a Colon

Number. It is T2 :44. Here

T	= Education	is Main Class
2	= Secondary education	is a division in the Educand schedule
44	= Curriculum	is a number in the Problem schedule
:		is the connecting symbol prescribed

The facet-formula prescribes the order in which the above symbols should be synthesised. Thus we get an individualising, co-extensive number, *i.e.*, a precise translation for the name of the specific subject. To use the old analogy of visitors and chairs, the Colon Classification can produce a greater abundance of chairs than the Decimal Classification. The occasions when two visitors will be obliged to sit on the same chair will be few and far between. Indeed the ideal is to eliminate such an occasion altogether. The further equipment needed in the Colon Classification to realise that ideal will be gone into in chapter 18.

16110 Uniqueness of Translation

There is one danger in an analytico-synthetic classification when viewed as language. Since an enumerative classification gives a ready-made translation (class number) made by the classificationist himself, it is ensured that no two different translations are made for the same original (specific subject). But it is well known that when different translators translate with the aid of a dictionary, they may produce different translations. This is perhaps a desirable feature in literary translation. But it will be disastrous in classificatory translation. For, translating the name of a given specific subject into two different class numbers will mean inconsistency in arrangement.

That is why it has been stated that an essential quality of a classificatory language is that it must have no synonym and two different translations for the same original passage should not be allowed or possible. It is the facet-formula which protects Colon Classification from this potential danger. It is that formula which gives the necessary rigidity. But we have to beware that the facet-formula does not introduce more rigidity than it is absolutely necessary for avoiding synonyms. If it introduces a greater amount of rigidity than it is necessary, to that extent it will restrict the potential vocabulary of the classificatory language. This again will be examined in chapter 18.

1612 ANALOGY OF CARTOGRAPHY

To get a view of the map of the field of knowledge provided by the Colon Classification one must take into consideration fully worked-out class numbers, past, present and future. If that is done it will be found that a good map is provided. The conscious implementation of Hospitality in Chain and Hospitality in Array in the methodology of the Colon Classification, keeps co-ordinate classes and subordinate classes quite apart as and when new areas (specific subjects) are explored and have to be marked on the map. The facet-notation enables the Colon Classification to carry out these obligations of cartographers even more thoroughly than the Decimal Classification is able to do.

1613 ANALOGY WITH TRANSFORMATION

Viewing the problem from the angle of analogy with transformation, the facet and the phase-notation of the Colon Classification enables it to avoid the fault of the Decimal Classification described in section 1523. It is not merely the end sub-cell in the multi-dimensional space of the field of knowledge, which is transformed into the end sub-interval in the linear space of class numbers, which is fully represented. But every one of the sub-cells in a cluster constituting a compound cell is rightly transformed.

1614 ANALOGY WITH BOOLEAN ALGEBRA

In using the terminology of the Boolean Algebra the field of Colon Numbers is a closed one in the sense that the product of any two sub-fields is contained within the total field. By throwing the search light of Boolean Algebra on the Colon Classification, it is expected that some of the subtler faults which are escaping unnoticed may be brought to light.

1615 ANALOGY WITH STATECRAFT

The notation of the Colon Classification is even more resourceful in its counter-tactics than that of the Decimal Classification. It has been able to withstand the grosser attacks of the field of knowledge. But in our days the field of knowledge has started, as it were, bacteria warfare. It has begun to play Hanuman's tactics as described in section 1515. It is playing these tactics unendingly. Just as the vocal muscle of the witch in the *Ramayana* episode became too stiff at a certain stage for the jaws to be easily moved, we have been experiencing that the rigidity of the facet-formula is causing trouble in putting up the necessary counter-tactics. It is to take away this rigidity that the work on Optional Facets is being pursued. This will be referred to in chapter 18.

1616 OTHER ANALOGIES

The Colon Classification has virtually no patent medicine. Every mixture has to be compounded according to prescriptions written out by a competent doctor to meet the exact requirement of the disease diagnosed. This does no mean that mixtures in frequent demand should not be compounded and stored in advance to be handed over readily on demand.

Similarly the Colon Classification has virtually no ready-made toys. Every toy should be built up to suit the exact fancy of the child needing it. This does not mean that the toys in frequent demand should not be assembled in advance and kept in readiness, to be handed over readily on demand

1617 OPTICAL ANALOGY AND TERMINOLOGY.

As it has been stated in section 147 that the Colon Classification has closely followed the optical analogue in the design of its terminology, there is no need to elaborate further the statements made in that section. The structure of the Colon Number discloses more fully than any other classification number the structure of the specific subject.

1618 INFINITE HOSPITALITY

A new feature of the Colon Classification which, however, needs to be mentioned here concerns the method it uses: (1) to secure theoretically infinite Hospitality in Array and in Chain severally.

16181 Hospitality in Array

To secure Infinite Hospitality in Array the Colon Classification uses not only the Octave Notation (described in section 13911) but also other devices like Subject Device, Alpbahetical Device, Geographical Device and Chronological Device. These are all described and illustrated in the *Colon classification*. Of these, it is the Chronological Device which has unusual facility to provide truly Infinite Hospitality in Array. It has stood the test admirably in accommodating Authors in Literature with neat individualising class numbers, no matter how many they are. It is also showing its capacity in individualising any number of special schools of thought in any region of knowledge. In the former, it consists in representing an author by the year of his birth. This makes classification of the authors belonging to any particular form of literature in any particular language chronological. This arranges the works by and on them in a manner which is not only helpful, in the ordinary sense, but also suggests the evolution of the literary art. I have experienced with great delight the unusual help which students of literature have derived by the arrangement of books in Literature with the aid of this device.

16182 Hospitality in Chain

It has been already stated that Hospitality in Chain is got by the decimal-fraction-notation which imitates the denudation process by which the links in the chain are successively derived.

16183 Unscheduled Mnemonics

When a link (immediate universe) begins to throw forth its links of higher order, it often happens that all the links in the array of the next order are not thrown out at one time. If they are, it may be easy to determine a 'more or less helpful' arrangement among them and allot the extra digit or digits needed to represent them according to the octave notation or any of the devices mentioned above. When they are not thrown out at one time, it is difficult to surmise which place the first link which is thrown out should be given in the array—which octave and which place in the octave. It is here that the Colon Classification has contributed what has been described in the *Prolegomena* as Unscheduled Mnemonics. It is a subtle device and is therefore a powerful one. It gives a greater degree of autonomy to a classifier in sharpening Simple and Dependent Foci. It is difficult to explain it in general terms though it has been attempted in the *Philosophy of library classification* (now being published in Copenhagen). Unscheduled Mnemonics consists in using an ordinal digit to represent a primordial idea which is not often represented by any term in a natural language, when it is taken in isolation, but is represented by different terms when it is put in the context of the different subjects. For example, the digit 3 represents Physiology in Biological Sciences, Social practices in Sociology, Functions of State in Political Science, Teaching Technique in Education, Distribution in Economics, Contract in Legal System and so on—all at bottom analogous at least in a thin or distant way. This mnemonic quality enables a classifier to form new foci in any facet without reference to the classificationist. What is more he need not wait to give numbers to these foci until all of them have appeared. Even when only one appears, he can number it with a high probability that it need not be changed and that very other classifier and the classificationist himself would be numbering it in the same way. The organisational set up on national and international basis for removing the effect of the small probability for inconsistency in fixing numbers by unscheduled mnemonics, has been described in *Library classification and international documentation* (1948) which appeared in the *Review of documentation* of the F. I. D. I have some vague information that there is a tradition of such unscheduled mnemonics current in the Tantric school. I wish something is done to collect, record and study this tradition of unscheduled mnemonics. Even among the common folk in western countries there is some trace of this which is brushed aside as sheer superstition. But scientific outlook requires that we should not brush aside anything on the sole ground that we cannot fit it into the rational matrix which intellect produces. We should be prepared to postulate and even grant trans-intellectual existents, though it is necessary to be on our guard not to become credulous subjects of fraud.

164 Universal Decimal Classification

The first scheme with an analytico-synthetic element was the Universal Decimal Classification. Though the Universal Decimal Classification was not accessible at the time when the Colon Classification was designed and consequently it has not been possible to use it as a model in the designing of the Colon Classification, there is no denying that the latter appeared in the field only a generation later. In spite of it, it had been taken first for description because it has developed the features of an analytico-synthetic classification in a more pronounced and fundamental manner and the auxiliary books and writings centering round it have developed a terminology which makes communication easier. It was a good in disguise that the schedules of Universal Decimal Classification were not accessible for several years after the Colon Classification was designed and developed up to the third edition. If it had been, the pressure of its tradition would have inhibited free thought, even as the Decimal Classification had done. Indeed, it is being realised that many of the faults of the Colon Classification are due to the pressure of the tradition of the Decimal Classification.

One of the reasons for the Universal Decimal Classification being unable to get the full benefit of an analytico-synthetic scheme is its adoption of a rigid core—that of the Decimal Classification which is essentially of the enumerative kind as shown in section 152 and its sub-divisions, and of the mere grafting to it of an analytico-synthetical element. This matter has been more fully elaborated in the *Self-perpetuating scheme of classification* (1949) published in the *Journal of documentation* of the ASLIB.

The rigidity of the Decimal Classification core has not only clipped the wings of the Universal Decimal Classification in the design of its numbers but has also prevented it from hitting upon something like Unscheduled Mnemonics and enunciating proper rules for the construction of class numbers.

What is more serious, it has been prevented from exploiting the linguistic analogue. It has failed to see that an artificial language of ordinal numbers designed for mechanising arrangement, which it is, would be doing a fatal mistake if it admitted synonyms. It has deliberately admitted synonyms by describing that the members on two sides of a colon may be interchanged without any change in meaning. To use the terminology of Boolean Algebra, it makes multiplication of facets commutative whereas it must be kept non-commutative.

The tradition of the rigid Decimal Classification core has also made it insensitive to the havoc that homonyms can play in a classificatory language. In fact, they create in little the very chaos which classification is expected to eliminate. They produce several little pockets, all through the scheme, of foggy classes in which several units of thought get arranged at random without any respect to helpfulness—and what is more— even to consistency.

In a paper entitled *Does Colon point the way?* published in the *Proceedings* of the Sixth All India Library Conference held at Jaipur in 1944, B. I. Palmer has analysed the futility of the methods available for making the Decimal Classification core to keep step with the movements in the field of knowledge. Himself and Mr. A. J. Wells are now bringing out a book, *Fundamentals of classification*, in which they make some positive suggestion.

It is high time that the classificationist-personnel and the classificatory-effort, which are all too small, should be better co-ordinated as an international enterprise to make library classification as efficient as possible. It should also be made progressive and totally free from rigidity of any kind. It should be fitted to meet what has been already referred to in section 1615 as the 'bacterial warfare' which the field of knowledge has begun to practise. A truly analytico-synthetic classification with provision, theoretically, for any number of facets and all possible varieties of phases appears to be the one possible weapon with which the new tactics of the field of knowledge can be met.

CHAPTER 17

Uses of Analytico-Synthetic Classification

We have seen that classification began even in prehistoric times and as a neural necessity, as the arrangement of the existents of the universe of discourse in an order ' more or less helpful.' We then traced the necessity for defining library classification as extending the original definition of classification so as to include the setting up of a system of ordinal numbers to denote the existents in order to mechanise their arrangement. We also examined the implications of the field of knowledge being infinite and finally arrived at the need for an analytico-synthetic classification. Before getting into an examination of all the implications of such a classification, it may be well to take stock of the uses to which it can be put.

171 Original Use

For the completeness of the enumeration of uses, we may repeat as the first use of an analytico-synthetic classification the original use for which library classification was forged. It is the mechanisation of the arrangement of all kinds of specific subjects—in reality the reading and kindred materials embodying them or entries describing the latter.

172 Help to Classifiers

A second use of an analytico-synthetic classification is its provision of clear-cut matrices to help the discovery and the enunciation by the classifier, of the specific subject of a reading or kindred material by a correct canalisation. Its facet- and phase-formulae act somewhat like the resonators used in analysing sound waves or like the spectrometers used in analysing waves of radiation. Yes, thought-waves too need some such aid in their analysis. The facet- and phase-formulae are of immense help to the classifier at the first stage of his work—the formulation of the name of the specific subject of a reading or kindred material, in standard terms in the preferred natural language. It guides him in looking for, breaking down into, and picking out, the fundamental constituent concepts of which a specific subject is composed. In othet words, it canalises his construction of the specific subject.

1721 ENUMERATIVE CLASSIFICATION AS BEACON LIGHT

We can see the additional advantage which an analytico-synthetic classification gives to the classifier over and above what an enumerative classification can do, with the aid of the following analogy. Compare a classifier to a person working his way through a forest during night time towards the home of his host (specific subject) who lives somewhere in the heart of the forest. The difficulties, the uncertainties, the frustration due to difficult terrain—treacherous with its hillocks, valleys, unfordable streams, uncrossable ditches, unscaleable terraces and so on—, the absence of a guide to the direction in which the home of the host lies and the multitudinous division of pathways, the sign-posts at which are invisible on account of the darkness of the night, all these will be similar to the traveller and the classifier. But suppose the host puts up a powerful lamp at the top of his house, so that it is visible from a distance. Then it will act as a beacon and minimise the trials of the traveller. Any good enumerative scheme of classification gives a similar help to the classifier in working his way towards the specific subject of the reading and kindred materials.

1722 ANALYTICO-SYNTHETIC CLASSIFICATION AS SEARCH-LIGHT

The traveller will be helped much more, saved many wrong turns and attracted to the home more easily, if the light put up by the host is a searchlight which not only acts as a beacon but also lights up the region through which he has to walk. Then will not merely the goal be glimmering but every inch of the way will be illuminated. The formula of facets and phases of a well-designed analytico-synthetic scheme of classification will serve the purpose of such a light to the classifier.

173 Help to Reference Librarians and Readers

A third use of an analytico-synthetic scheme of classification also stems from its capacity for correct canalisation. It helps the joint exploration by a reference librarian and a reader of the requirements of the reader and in the exact enunciation of the specific subject on which he wants materials and the auxiliary subjects which also should be brought to his notice. In *Reference service and bibliography* (1940) many case-studies have been recorded illustrating the way in which an analytico-synthetic classification helps in this process. To get the fullest benefit it is necessary that ready-made class numbers with their equivalents in natural language should be spread out before the reader. This is virtually done by the guide-cards or the feature-headings of the classified part of the catalogue derived from class number by chain procedure. These throw before the reader's eyes an ordered panorama of all related subjects when he glances through that panorama.

1731 FAILURE TO NAME SPECIFIC SUBJECT

He is able to pick out the exact subject which he has been longing to name but he had not. He had not because perhaps he was unable to do so. Yes, even in the case of very erudite readers occasions often arise when they could not enunciate their specific subjects. Witness the illustrative actualities given in chapter 34 of *Reference service and bibliography.* It also happens, equally often, that he had not stated his specific subjects exactly, though he knew it, because he did not expect that the library would have made a class of it or that the librarian would be learned enough to recognise it.

1732 HELP OF CLASSIFIED DISPLAY

Whatever the reason, the orderly display of specific subjects provided by an analytico-synthetic classification coupled with chain procedure gives to a reader the same kind of help as an orderly display of articles in a shop does to a customer. No doubt, open-access does this to considerable extent. But even there it is classified arrangement or display that manages it. Moreover, the guide-cards and feature-headings of the classified part of a catalogue reproduce the panorama within a much shorter range, fit to be taken by the eye in a single glance.

1733 SHIFT IN EMPHASIS

This experience of reference librarians on floor-duty points out a shift in the emphasis of classification. Arrangement on shelf is no longer the sole purpose. It is only one of the purposes. The other two services enumerated above for the classifier and the reader have even a greater potency than the original use. It is the failure to recognise this shift in emphasis, the failure to view an analytico-synthetic classification as a tool for the search of the specific subject of a writing or of the specific subject in the reader's mind, that is responsible for inadequate attention to the classificatory technique.

174 Help to Documentation

1741 WHAT IS DOCUMENTATION

A fourth use of an analytico-synthetic classification is in its potentiality to render exactly and expeditiously what has in recent years been termed 'Documentation Work and Service.' This new term has been coined to emphasise the deeper phase into which reference service entered about half a century ago in the United States and about twenty-five years ago in Europe. It is on the eve of entering India and other Asian countries. This phase first made its appearance in business libraries—libraries of industrial houses, commercial houses, government departments and newspaper offices. During the last decade this phase has also been entering public and academic libraries, though in a halting manner. The distinguishing feature of this phase of reference service is the spotting out of all published materials on micro-units of for specialist thought.

These have to be searched for in ephemeral leaflets, pamphlets, reprints, articles in periodicals and newspapers and in odd pages of books. They have to be described and their descriptions have to be assembled together and featured in a short compass. This has to be done to meet the most exacting demands of the First Law in the form 'Documents are for use,' the Second Law in the form 'Every user his documents,' and the Third Law in the form 'Every document its user.' The Fourth and Fifth Laws combine together to put the reference librarian to the severest test possible. The number of periodical publications has increased during the last half a century from a few thousand to many hundreds of thousands. Articles embodying micro-units of thought are being produced in millions every year. The formation of the micro-units of thought is largely by the lamination and loose assemblage of a multitude of facets and phases which bring several disciplines into inter-relation. It is conjectured that the latter is becoming dominant in our days. This has been provisionally verified by K. D. Puranik in his article *Field of knowledge and its repercussions in classification* published in *Abgila*, V. 2, 1951. March, pp. 1—24. The Fourth Law demands that this downpour of variegated materials should be sorted out and the right ones should be picked out for a user without any loss of time. This is documentation work.

1742 FAILURE OF DOCUMENTALISTS

It is regretable that those who practice documentation work and service have not fully realised the great help which an analytico-synthetic classification can give to them. It is pathetic to see them struggling to serve with the outmoded, unhelpful, cumbersome tool of subject-headings. These scatter subjects in a most ruthless way. They tire out readers even if it is contended that they do not hide the materials themselves. The failure on the part of so-called special librarians is traceable to historical causes. In the past, library classification has been largely developed by public-librarians who had only the necesssity to handle micro-units of thought embodied in books and more often requisitioned for relaxation and inspiration rather than for information on the latest wave-front of knowledge in its diverse regions. Consequently, library classification came to be frozen in their hands at the stage of enumerative classification. The industrial and commercial houses, whose success depended on specialised information which is of the latest brand, felt the need for service of micro-units of thought. They had only the scientists and technologists themselves to draw from for his service. For though they did not know the discipline of classification, their familiarity with their own narrow field of specialisation made them do a better job than a librarian with neither specialisation nor the help of a more powerful classification than the enumerative one. These subject-specialists were too pre-occupied with their specialisation and offered resistance to take up the sharpening of the classificatory tool.

1743 HOPEFUL SIGN

But there is every evidence—the Royal Society's Conference of 1948 is one of them—that there is an increasing volume of opinion that the situation could no longer be met unless a strong profession of documentalists is set up and unless they forge a powerful classificatory technique to sift, organise, and produce on demand, micro-units of thought. This is a hopeful sign. It will be more productive if it is realised that their organisation and the make-up and display of their list should be such as to enable the consumer to sense easily all that may be relevant to his needs. An analytico-synthetic classification indicates one of the directions in which that technique is to be sought.

175 Help to Communication

A fifth use of an analytico-synthetic classification which has been recently suggested is in the field of communication—particularly international communication. This is a new use which has to be investigated. This is a use which has become urgent. The urgency is caused by historical fact. During the last two centuries most of the creative thinking used English, French and German as the media. It was not difficult for creative mind to be at home in three languages—especially these three near-cousins. But today there is an awakening and an ebullition of creative thought in many parts of the world. The Slav languages have already become important media for new thought since the First World War. The end of the Second World War has released minds who can think most effectively in the Sanskritic, Semetic, Dravidian and the East Asian languages. The world can ill afford to make several linguistic groups re-do what has been done elsewhere. There is need for the happenings in the wave-front of knowledge recorded in any language of the world to be communicated unerringly and without any delay to the minds which can resonate with it, in spite of their languages of thinking being different. This is a vital problem in international communication. This points to the need for examining international communication and the part that an artificial language like the classificatory one can play in it and the modifications that the classificatory language should undergo to make it fit for use in international communication. With this in view, part 2 will be first devoted to examine communication in all its aspects in relation to co-operative living on a world scale. Then will follow part 3 linking up classification and communication and examining its effect on classificatory thought and research.

CHAPTER 18

Depth-Classification—Confession of Faith

In the earlier chapters we have seen frequently that the direction in which classification, in the third sense, should be taken is that of increasing minuteness. Enumerative classification proves unfit to be taken in that direction. Even a hybrid, enumerative *cum* analytico-synthetic classification soon loses its fitness. It is only a pure analytico-synthetic classification that can stand the strain of minute classification. We have also seen that there are three means of sharpening focus, *i.e.*, of building co-extensive individualising class numbers. One of them is the sharpening of Dependent Foci. Another is increasing the number of Facets to be laminated and making multi-laminated Compound Foci. The third is recognising new kinds of phases, designing distinctive connecting symbols for them, in short making multi-phased Complex Foci. The first of these is fairly well provided for by decimal-fraction-notation and unscheduled mnemonics which, of course, needs further objectivisation. The last presents comparatively fewer problems to be faced.

131 Optional Facet Notation

Therefore, the success of the further sharpening of over-all foci, *i.e.*, of depth-classification, really depends on increasing the number of facets. This bristles with difficulties. The setting up of optional-facet-notation, the designing of signature-digits and the building up of 120 or 2,400 primordial schedules which are variant manifestations of the fundamental categories— Time, Space, Energy, Matter, and Personality—mentioned in section 1371, appear to be one of the methods which may yield the desired result. Considerable team-work is necessary to develop these methods. This will be provided for by society only if the elite realise the need for depth-classification—the elite in the library profession in the first instance and the elite among the statesmen of the world necessarily.

182 Depth Classification

I therefore conclude this part which is on classification with my confession of faith in this matter of close or depth-classification. It may be described as close because, in the final result, the class number closely fits the specific subject, is co-extensive with it and individualises it. It may be called depth-classification because it carries the exploration of the intension of the specific subject to the deepest level possible and, for this purpose, has to employ analysis of the greatest penetration and depth.

183 Why ?

Why does a librarian classify at all ? Why should he practise depth-classification ? He classifies and should practise depth-classification to uncover to himself, in order to make it readily available to the appropriate reader, everything, however minute, which the library has on anything—all the micro-units of thought which have been expressed and embodied. It is true that comparatively few devote any time at all to practical depth-classification. But those who practise reference service would agree that the resources uncovered by depth-classification are extremely important to know and the deeper the classification the greater the uncovering of the resources. This raises the question: " Why so many do not practise depth-classification ? "

184 Why not ?

Some do not classify closely because it embarrasses them to try to be as serious as depth-classification demands. Others disbelieve in the sincerity of the classificationist and feel that they affect a humanly impossible seriousness. Then there are those who have a vague goodwill towards classificationists and depth-classification, but who feel that the rewards are small compared with the amount of time and energy necessary—that depth-classification is much too hard work.

Some have a natural disinclination to classify closely, which deserves to be respected. For, we respect those who, conscious that they lack the proper qualification of experience or judgment, modestly refrain from advancing opinions on controversial subjects.

But there are also some who, from their education and sensibility, might be expected to practise depth-classification and yet do not. The strongest single reason why they do not is mis-education as to the reasons of classification. They have acquired either the impression that depth-classification yields only a fanciful kind of result, or amounts to nothing more than an academic exercise, or means mere metaphysical conceit ; or they have the impression that all the benefits of depth-classification can be obtained more easily by other ordinary means such as the dictionary-catalogue to which tradition has accustomed them, without recourse to depth-classification which involves the tediousness of reading the materials through and finding all their facets and the dependent foci in them in their accurate forms or degrees of sharpness.

But no librarians except those who insist on classifying for the wrong reason should find depth-classification too complicated or too difficult or too tedious. No librarians who classify for the right reason should find it anything but proper, helpful and worthwhile. But what are the right reasons for classification? Do most librarians who classify broadly or superficially do so for wrong reasons? Is a scheme of classification, which does not aim at closeness or depth but finds a large number of practitioners, likely to have been designed for wrong reasons?

185 What?

Classification is an uncovering of the thought-content of a written or expressed unit of thought. In all its minutest details it is what it should be only when the thought-content as a whole is uncovered including all the phases, facets and foci by those faculties which apprehend all the details exhaustively and yet in terms of entirety rather than in terms merely of parts. It is only an analytico-synthetic scheme that can uncover thought-content in such a holistic way. The classificationist who designs a scheme for the right reasons has felt the need for such a scheme and for the exercise of such faculties; and he has himself such faculties. The classifier who applies a classification scheme for the right reasons will ask the classificationist to provide him in the scheme of classification with aids to accentuate these faculties and exercise them. The reference librarian too will ask the classificationist to do similarly. For he too is a classifier in another sphere. For he has to make the result of classifying materials reach its right destiny ; for this purpose, he has to apprehend all the details of readers' demand exhaustively and holistically ; in fact he applies the classification scheme in the ultimate stage of library service which is effecting contact between the right reader and the right unit of thought in a personal way.

186 Corrupted Reason

But corruption of the reason of classification sets in—in both the classificationist and the classifier—when the classifier goes to classification with no notion whatever of the faculties required. The history of designing classification and classifying is in large part a history of such corruption.

To-day corruption of values is responsible for regression to broad classification, even to abandonment of classification and open access, and so-called compact-shelving confusing issues, as if saving shelf-space is the ultimate *summum bonum* of library service. It is corruption of values which resists progression towards depth-classification. Corruption is like weeds. It spreads speedily and extensively. Right values get smothered. Men with right values have to face ridicule if not stoning. Thank God, prison bars, hemlock and the cross do not come into the library world. The facile incidence of corruption of values, is because of the visible effects of wrong and right modes not being immediate but deferred. The pitiable extent to which corruption of values can occult judgment is pictured in Milton's *Comus* :—

> And they, so perfect is their misery,
> Not once perceive their foul disfigurement,
> But boast themselves more comely than before,
> And all their friends and native home forget,
> To roll with pleasure in a sensual sty.

The depravity with which corruption of values tempts those with right values is described with subtle humour in Valmiki's *Ramayana.* The demon Surpaṇakha told Rama :—

> सुमुखं दुर्मुखी रामं वृत्तमध्यं महोदरी ।
> विशालाक्षं विरूपाक्षी सुकेशं ताम्रमूर्धजा ॥
> प्रियरूपं विरूपा सा सुस्वरं भैरवस्वना ॥
> तरुणं दारुणा वृद्धा दक्षिणं वामभाषिणी ॥
> न्यायवृत्तं सुदुर्वृत्ता प्रियम् अप्रियदर्शना ।
> शरीरजसमाविष्टा राक्षसी राममब्रवीत् ॥
> "विकृता च विरूपा च न सेयं सदृशी तव ।
> इमां विरूपाम् असतीं करालां निर्णतोदरीम् ।
> अनेन सह ते भ्रात्रा भक्षयिष्यामि मानुषीम्" ॥

> Rama had a cheerful face ; the demon-woman
> had an evil look.
> His waist was slim ; she was pot-bellied.
> Rama was broad-eyed ; she was squint-eyed.
> His hair was fine ; hers was copper-coloured.
> Rama was handsome ; she was shapeless.
> He had a pleasant voice ; hers was harsh.
> Rama was a youth ; she was a hag.
> He was considerate in his talk ; she was foul.
> Rama was righteous ; she was very wicked.
> He was endearing ; she was repulsive.

In a fit of brute-passion, that demon told Rama about Sita, his consort (who was the very ideal of beauty and charm according to human standards).

"This woman of yours is deformed and ugly. She is no worthy partner to you. I shall devour this ugly, wicked frightful woman slim at waist along with that brother of yours."

187 Right Reason

Reference service is too recent to speak of its history. It is done in the immediate presence of the readers in the inexorable grip of a nascent mental urge, unlike the work of the classificationist and classifier which is done behind the screen without the compulsion of the immediate presence of readers. Reference service, it is believed, cannot therefore be prone to similar corruption. If this be true, the drive for depth-classification will come from reference librarians and that will be for the right reason.

The right reason for classification is that it helps us to know readers and to know reading and kindred materials, in and out, and match them—particularly the readers who extend the boundaries of the field of knowledge and dig deep into it, and the materials which embody the micro-units of nascent thought in the very wave-front of knowledge. We should not feel shy of either. We should take our mission as establishing contact between reader of that sort and reading materials of that sort, exactly, exhaustively, expeditiously and without any fumbling. We shall then see that no scheme of classification can be too close or too deep or too complicated or too exacting to be worthwhile.

We shall also see that the reader is no more concerned with the notational part of classification in the third sense, or of the how of classificatory technique except in its very superfices, no more concerned than a passenger is with the air-engine or of the how of its working except in its very superfices. The service of depth-classification can reach the reader in difficult situations and in its deepest reaches only through the reference librarian ; in other words, classification in its deepest embellishment has to be intelligible only to the reference librarian, though an intelligent reader may be prepared to share it with him. It can even be said and it will be experienced that the extent to which a reader contacts the profound possibilities of fully expressive, co-extensive, class numbers, will be proportional to the depth and the profoundness of the thought he seeks to feed upon, from among the materials which the library has or the world produces.

If these are conceded, it will be realised that what should be aimed at is translating the entire thought-content of an embodied or expressed thought—all its dependent foci in the fullest degree of their sharpness, all its criss-cross of concepts and forms and all its interlacings—fully and literally into ordinal numbers whose structure lays bare all such foci, criss-crosses and interlacings. This is depth-classification.

188 Confession of Faith

My faith is that it is only an analytico-synthetic classification that can stand the strain of depth-classification. It is necessary if we are to effect total integration between reading and kindred materials and readers. My faith is that a library—*granthalaya*—exists only at moments when a purposive, effective, holistic participation takes place between reading materials, readers and reference librarians and thereby total integration takes place between reading and kindred materials and readers. Libraries in this sense—the only correct sense—are necessary to promote communication. My faith is that promotion of world-wide communication is necessary to radiate happiness, joy and delight.

Part 2

Communication

CHAPTER 21

Co-operative Living

Life in society differs from jungle life. Life is lived co-operatively in society. There is a pooling of knowledge in human society at all levels, through all ages, and across all space. A human being is never solely dependent on his own experience for his information, intellection or inspiration.

211 Co-operative Life at all Levels

Co-operative life pervades all levels—vital, mental and spiritual. Even some beasts have learnt to co-operate with advantage at the vital level. Even primitive man had learnt to co-operate with advantage at the mental level. The Vedic tradition and the literary evidence of ancient poems like the *Ramayana* refer to co-operation at the unspeakable level of mysticism and spiritual experience.

2111 Vital Level

In the vital level of attending to bodily needs, we find advantage in living co-operatively. The necessary food, clothing and shelter are procured more easily and in greater abundance if we seek them in co-operation. We have found by experience that ten people working for the supply of vital needs, in utter isolation of one another, achieve much less than what they do if they work in co-operation. Man need not live on man or at the cost of other men. It is true that the distribution of the fruits of co-operative living is not always equitable. It is true that there are springs in human personality from which terrible selfishness flows. When selfishness and cleverness go together science is travestied to justify failure to be equitable. Analogy is drawn from jungle life and it is posed " In nature one lives on another. There is more of it than of co-operation. The law of the survival of the fittest rules. And so on." No doubt beasts have had to live on other beasts. But they were mostly beasts of other species. This analogy cannot therefore hold among humans who all belong to the same species. Apart from the fallacy of invoking pseudo-science to justify unnatural acts, there is a trace in man of the urge to live the opposite of co-operative life. One projection of this urge into our present age is what is politely called " Competitive life." In this the extent of co-operation is restricted in varying degrees—to nations, groups, families, and even individuals. In some cases, fear inhibits co-operation and promotes conflicts, strike and war. Despite all this, there is no denying that there is a huge substratum of co-operation which keeps the world going. The satisfaction of certain emotional urges set up by the glandular system is impossible if we do not co-operate.

2112 Mental Level

The desire to know is inherent in man. This desire too is satisfied to a greater extent if knowledge is sought by a team working in concert than by one working for ever in solitude. Even the most creative mind seeks co-operation of others, though at a lower mental level, to enable their own creative potentiality to fulfil itself. Indeed, the Vedic definition of education insists on four stages, the first and the fourth of which are by definition impossible in isolation. For they say that education is a process which begins with imitation by and learning from a teacher, and needs for its completion initiation of and teaching to a student.

2113 SPIRITUAL LEVEL

When a man's spiritual potentiality manifests itself, he gets into intimate, sympathetic at-one-ment with everybody else and everything else in the universe. His co-operation extends over all space and all time. Co-operation is indeed supreme. There is no alternative. It is inevitable. Whatever he does he is perfectly participative. This is the burden of the song in the *Divine utterance* of India called the *Bhagavad Gita.*

2114 VEDIC TESTIMONY

Thus material happiness, mental joy and spiritual delight are each realised better by working in co-operation with others than in isolaton. Well did the Rig Vedic seers sing:

> Move together, talk together, understand aright.
> Deliberate together, achieve together,
> Remember in common, think in co-operation.
> Alike be your intentions, harmonious your feelings,
> And concerted your thoughts,
> So that there may be complete co-operation among you.

212 Mental Heritage

Humanity has now advanced well into the mental age. It is long since it emerged from the age of instinct, when its existence, activity and mutual relations were regulated solely by hormones and biochemical forces without the intervention of deliberate mental action. He is no longer a mere colony of aggregates of cells of protoplasm. The development of the brain and particularly its cortical region has made him in a sense master of biochemistry instead of biochemistry being his master. This has enabled him to live in co-operation even with his dead ancestors. The departed live *in absentia*, so to speak, with the living. The living and the dead work in a co-operative chain at the mental level. The result is that mental heritage is more lasting and cumulative than material heritage. Mental joy is less dependent on pragmatic realisaton than spiritual delight. This makes mental heritage more easily cumulative and transmitive than spiritual heritage.

2121 PROGRESS AND EXTERNALISED MEMORY

So far as mental progress is concerned the living begin where the dead left. Human progress depends on this. It is made possible by the capacity of the human mind to externalise memory, so to speak, and leave it behind even when the body dies. Memory is so externalised that the succeeding generation can make it its own and by-pass the need to acquire all that by its own effort starting from scratch. This is not possible for beasts. This capacity to benefit by mental heritage leads to a perpetually swelling confluence of mental heritage.

2122 INTENSIVE CO-OPERATION

This confluence of mental heritage helps and intensifies co-operative living at all the levels—vital, mental and spiritual. It demands, leads to, and makes possible a more extensive co-operative life at all the three levels. This perennial self-enrichment of mental heritage has been repeatedly painted in parables in some of the timeless poems like the *Ramayana*, *Mahabharatha* and of *Bhagavata*.

2123 MIXEDNESS OF MENTAL HERITAGE

It must however be remembered that everything which is inherited is not of equal value. Mental heritage is like Pandora's box. Co-operative living is necessary to avoid its dangers. Deliberation, evaluation, and judgment as to what part of mental heritage is outmoded and therefore poisonous, what part will endure eternally, and what part will be serviceable at present though not in future—to discriminate and judge all these—working in co-operation is essential.

213 Towards One World

Let us define a Territorial Unit as that extent of territory which can form the abode of a closed unit of co-operative living.

Co-operative living with ever-increasing mental heritage has been leading to a progressive extension of the area of territorial unit. This extension is a concomitant of the co-operative living practised by man. It has enabled him to satisfy his physical and mental wants, withstand diseases, and thereby extend the average span of life. This has been progressively leading to an excess of birth over death—to an increase in population. Increase in population results in the disturbance of the balance between the needs of the people occupying a territory and its capacity to meet such needs. Population-pressure overreaches, as it is put. When this happens, pockets of people living in isolation as closed units are obliged to spread out until the boundary of one pocket touches that of another. Then the two communities eventually get coalesced and get integrated into a bigger pocket of co-operative living, occupying a larger area. The territorial unit becomes larger.

2131 FORMATION OF NATION

Time was when the family determined the territorial unit of co-operative living. When the number of families in a given area multiplied beyond a certain limit, the orbits of several families intersected. In the first instance this often led to clash and strife. But soon the families learnt the wisdom of co-operative living. Village-life set in. The territory of the closed unit of co-operation was extended to cover a village. The spheres for the individuality of the family and the co-operative living of the community were soon demarcated and the conflict between the two spheres were progressively eliminated. Thus the area of the territorial unit of co-operative living was firmly established in its extended measure. When the number of villages in a given area multiplied, the orbits of several village-communities intersected. In the first instance this often led to clash and struggle. But soon the village communities learnt the wisdom of co-operative living and assimilation. Tribal life set in. The area of the territorial unit of the closed unit of co-operation was extended to cover a tribal area. The spheres for the individuality of the village-community and the co-operative living of the clan or tribe were soon demarcated and the conflict between the two spheres were progressively eliminated. Thus the area of the territorial unit of co-operative living was extended. This progression has been going on. Closed national units have been formed. The earth's surface has now been partitioned into territorial units of larger size for the exclusive co-operative living of each of the nations. The occupation of unoccupied areas has been helped by the technological progress made possible by the very co-operative living within the nation. The family and the various sub-territorial and occupational and other groups are trying to reconcile their respective spheres of individuality with the sphere of life as a nation. Man has now learnt to reconcile his loyalties to several groups, to live in each of them simultaneously in a co-operative manner and thereby to find happiness, joy and delight for himself and peace for the nation as a whole.

We shall next consider the effect of population-pressure within a nation and percolation across national boundaries. The result of the migration of peoples across national boundaries had depended on the relative numerousness and cultural stamina of the local and the immigrant communities.

2131 ASSIMILATION

The evolution of India, till she went into deep and prolonged sleep a few centuries ago, demonstrates one possible happening. So long as the local and immigrant communities are equally virile and have sufficient confidence in the possibility and power of co-operative living, they get assimilated in a happy way. The individuality of the culture of either is not totally obliterated. The spheres of the constituent communities and that of national co-operative living are easily marked out. The living together of different cultural groups adds not only to their vital well-being and their mental development but also to the enrichment of spiritual life. When spiritual awareness reaches a sufficiently high pitch, even language is seen to be no nececessary individualising factor in a cultural or national group. Even religion —in the sense of creeds and rituals—is seen to be no necessary individualising factor. The hey-days of India in the past had demonstrated the possibility of fullness of co-operative living even by different linguistic and religious groups. That is the message of India's assimilation in succession of Syrians, Arabs and Persians. In a similar way, in India's hey-days Indians also got integrated with the communities in Asia Minor in the West like those of Palestine and with the communities in South Asia like those of Ceylon, Indonesia, Malaya, Siam and Indo-China. In the eighteenth and nineteenth centuries India's exhaustion on the one hand and the resistance to assimilation offered by the Anglo-Saxon community on the other prevented a fully profitable co-operative living.

2133 COLONISATION

When the local community was too small in number or too weak in its cultural stamina, the pressure of the immigrant community led to its extinction. Witness the Red Indians and the Polynesians. When this happened, the area of migration was virtually equivalent to an unoccupied area. The result was colonisation.' 'Colonisation' is negation of co-operative living between the local and the immigrant communities. It is persistence of ruthless jungle-life. For some time the spreading out of the people of one nation into non-contiguous areas and colonising therein did not prevent the different sections from hanging on together and maintaining national affiliation by frequent exchange of people. Witness the British Colonial System. But eventually affiliation across the sea had weakened sooner or later and resulted in the formation of new nations. Witness the countries in North and South America.

2134 Empire Building

A third thing happened when a virile community was driven by population-pressure to migrate into other areas whose local commuity was weaker in its cultural stamina but was not extinguishable. In such cases exploitation was the result. Exploitation too is a negation of co-operative living. It too is jungle-life—one species living on another. If the original community is still tolerated and allowed to perpetuate itself and not extinguished, it is very much like cattle and beasts of burden being domesticated and husbanded. Empire is the result.

2135 An Index of the Future

Today the world is occupied almost fully. The communities in Asia and Africa are recovering from exhaustion. Freshness activates them. Exploiting nations are aging. Exhaustion is overtaking them. Consequently Empires are breaking down into independent nations. Colonies are also forming themselves into independent nations. Politically then the number of independent national groups is increasing. But economically, their orbits are getting criss-crossed. It looks as if national economics should yield to world-economics. World-economics means co-operative living over the entire face of the earth. But political traditions resist this tendency towards one world. Wars and conflagration are recurring rather too frequently. The area covered by war has always been a distant index of the size of the enlarged territorial unit of co-operative living which would be formed next. The fact that we have had two World Wars—*de juro* so and *de facto* nearly so—is a distant index of the fact that we are struggling towards World-State or Near-World-State. The failure of the League of Nations and the ineffectiveness of the United Nations no doubt show how much more difficult, arduous and tardy is the dawning of the wisdom that the time has come when the territorial unit for a closed unit of co-operation should be extended beyond that of a nation and that the spheres for the individuality of a nation and the co-operative living of the entire humanity should be discovered and implemented without conflict.

2136 Large Scale Mergers

The first merger on a large scale, the wisdom of which is being seen today, took place more than a century ago when the federation of the U.S.A. was put on a firm foundation. The U.S.S.R. is the second example. The formation of the Republic of India and the merger of the states within it is the most recent occurrence of comparable magnitude. All these countries have written constitutions which demarcate the spheres of the Union on the one side of the constituent States on the other. They show the possibility of coming to an agreement and enlarging the territorial unit of co-operative living. The formation of an enlarged nation by the merger of smaller nations was illustrated by the formation of the United Kingdom in the seventeenth century. On the other hand the attempt to merge the countries of Europe into a few larger units has failed so far. Will it ever be so ? Perhaps not.

2137 THE ULTIMATE GOAL

Neither the formation of large-scale nations by a federation of states nor the establishment of regional co-operative living can be the last word in the expansion of the territorial unit of co-operative living. So long as there are on the earth's surface even two closed units their orbits will ultimately begin to intersect. This will lead to a conflagration on a colossal scale. One-World should set in.

214 Militant Factors

2141 VISCOSITY OF POLITICAL LIFE

One of the factors which militate against the expansion of the territory of co-operative living to the entire surface of the earth is what may be called the viscosity of political life. As already stated, the force of this viscosity attempts to retain national boundaries in their restricted form and resist the force of economic necessity to cut across these boundaries and enlarge them to the point of their removal. Yet history of the past may perhaps be taken to indicate that the economic force will eventually overcome the viscosity of political life. It can be so taken unless it is proved that there is a critical upper-limit for the area within which co-operative living is possible. Past history does not throw any light on this question. We have therefore to be guided only by wish and faith. I for one wish and believe that there is no such upper-limit and that the entire face of the earth can eventually become a single territorial unit for co-operative living.

Some earlier resistances to the extension of the area of co-operative living have been totally or nearly eliminated. At first there was family strife. When it was eliminated, feudal strife set in. When this was eliminated, religious strife began its sway. It is true that in spite of religion (in the sense of creed and ritual) having outgrown the stage of being a true force either for co-operative living or for wars, its emotional capacity has been used by political forces to obstruct expansion and merger—alas, even to split up. This happened within living memory in Ireland and it happened the other day in India. Perhaps the world will use the slogan "Religion in danger" as a cover to protect political motives for some more time, but I believe not for ever. Resistance to merger is developing new roots in our own days. They call it ideological resistance. Resistance develops between different ideologies. "Democracy in danger" is one form which the slogan takes. "Down with capitalism" is another form. The world has yet to find some means of reconciling ideological differences with the economic need to extend the territorial unit to cover the whole earth. Influences of exceptional personalities are the only promoting factors which we can look up to at present. But these personalities cannot be produced to order.

2142 INSTITUTIONAL INERTIA

Another complex of obstruction to the extension of the area of the territorial unit of co-operative living may be described as the over-cementing done by the very urge for co-operation as it is developed within any one territorial unit or any one group. This over-cementing develops, as it were, an enveloping encrustation which resists merger with other groups. Sociologists call it 'institutional inertia.' Institution is an organised pattern of group behaviour brought about by co-operative living within the group. Once people get accustomed to an institution, they begin to feel that their institution represents the only right pattern of behaviour. It is true that we no longer say that it is of divine origin; but we do say and act as if we are convinced about its being the only proper one.

Institutions tend to stay long after the necessity for their existence disappear, and, often, even when their continued existence becomes a danger. All institutions do not have an equal period of usefulness. Some are of eternal value. Some become obsolete rapidly. But the cement and the encrustation harden equally in all. It is their hardened state in obsolete institutions which obstruct co-operative living being carried out in larger groups and territories. The obstruction due to institutional inertia may be increased by short-sighted selfishness, fear of change, and other psychological, social and ecological factors. Here again the peaceful breaking of institutional inertia can be brought about only by exceptional personalities.

2143 SPATIAL OBSTRUCTION

The very distance between nations and the physiographical barriers such as oceans, deserts and mountains—factors relating to sheer space have been militating against the expansion of the area of co-operative living. Technology is minimising the potency of such spatial obstructions. Rapid means of transport by land, water and air are dissolving space, as it were. The cost of transport too is being progressively reduced to make it feasible for an increasing number of members of different territorial units being mixed with those of others. Agencies like the British Council, measures like the Fulbright Act and the Smith-Mundt Act and Foundations like Carnegie, Rockefeller and Watumul are promoting cultural contact by providing for travel and exchange of nationals into and with other countries. Most of the individuals who have had experience of those organisations are convinced of their capacity to melt the political and cultural prejudices, suspicions and resistances engendered by mere spatial separation. Statistics of the activities of such organisations should be consolidated and widely disseminated by Unesco. Air transport, printing press and radio-waves make transmission and exchange of ideas both expeditious, and widespread. All these factors will in the long run disable space from obstructing the expansion of the territorial unit for co-operative living so as to cover the entire face of the earth.

215 Favourable Factor

There is however one favourable factor. The status of an individual in modern times derives from his relationship to new social forms which may be Functional Groups. His personality and his interests seek co-operation with other individuals in his own functional group. For the specificity of a person's intellectual interest is getting more and more intensified. It is thereby gaining more and more in strength so as to assert itself against biological and emotional interests which are more restrictive in nature. From the point of view of 'social engineering,' attention may, with profit, be directed to the promotion of co-operative mental living among members of a homogeneous group of intellectual interests. The establishment of scores of international specialist associations for the pursuit of physical, natural and social sciences is an index of the inherent urge in intellectuals for such a promotion. These groups of intellectual co-operative living first got formed within a localised community like that of a city, region or country. This accustomed people to co-operative living among those living in non-contiguous areas and having hardly any family or blood relationship or even ethnical similarity. The specificity has now got so intensified that many do not find their peers in necessary abundance even within a single country. They have to seek persons with whom they can intellectually resonate far outside their country. Thus the territorial area for the intellectual co-operative living is undergoing extra-local expansion. Confining ourselves to basic and applied sciences there are 261 international bodies and 34 regional bodies listed in Unesco's Directory of International Scientific Organisations (1950). The motive for co-operation among these world-wide and regional co-operative units is not religious, nor political or economic—in short not emotional. Nor is it biochemical or biological or ethnic. The motive is trans-emotional, trans-ethnic and intellectual. Emotional motives are centrifugal, subject to violent change, and intolerant. Ethnical motives are centripetal but intolerant. Intellectual motives on the other hand are centripetal, enduring and tolerant. An individual is born in an ethnic unit—often a closed unit. He has necessarily to belong to some emotional co-operative unit—particularly a nation—which is locally circumscribed. He also seeks to belong to some intellectual co-operative unit which cuts across boundaries of ethnical and emotional units and covers the whole earth. When strife develops between circumscribed ethnical or emotional units the co-operative living in the world-wide intellectual units goes under. This is due to the conservative character of ethnic bond and the capacity of emotion to develop more powerful binding force within the group, more powerful repelling force against other groups, and the forging of legal or other sanctions which are available to closed units of all sorts. These sanctions are usually deadly in their effect even if they are cold ones.

In spite of this, there is every hope that the intellectual binding force, which transcends territorial boundaries, will eventually gain in strength and lead to co-operative living on world-scale. Eventually! How distant? Measured in terms of an individual's average span of life, infinitely distant!! But in terms of the span of life of humanity as such, measurably distant!!! The human race is still in its infancy, characterised by explosive emotions and narrow exclusiveness. When it matures, eludes ethnic grips, develops control over emotions, becomes dominantly intellectual, and enters the supra-mental stage described by Sri Aurobindo, it will get glimpses of the delight of co-operative living in un-truncated, infinite context—the delight (=*Ananda*) which stray individuals have realised hitherto and denoted by the profound term Pure Existence *cum* Pure Consciousness *cum* Pure Delight, *Satchidananda*.

CHAPTER 22

Communication and Language

Even assuming that the centrifugal forces stemming from religious, political and economic motives of narrow egotism are either eliminated or subordinated by the centripetal force stemming from an intellectual motive of wide social value, the full exploitation of the situation will depend on the efficiency of communication. For, the building up of a unit of co-operative living will depend on the mutual understanding between its members. Understanding in its turn will depend on the process of communicacation. Indeed when we speak of an organised society, it is not a static structure defined by tradition that is meant. On the other hand, what is meant is a highly intricate network of mutual understanding. It may be understanding between individual members or groups of varying size and complexity in the territorial unit of co-operative living. It may be a pair of lovers or a family at one end of the scale and a nation or a family of nations at the other end. In between these two extremes, come the ever-increasing portion of humanity which can be reached through modern media like the printing press and radio broadcast. An organised society exists only as the flux of understanding maintained by communication between individuals and groups. In fact every single act of social behaviour involves communication of ideas and emotions in either an explicit or an implicit manner. Promotion of world-peace needs the extension of the territorial unit of closed co-operative living so as to cover the entire surface of the earth. These should be the objective of the sum-total of all the acts of social behaviour. These have to depend on communication. There should be persistent removal of the elements which block it. We should set up means of communication which will transmit ideas without obstruction, refraction, false addition or vague abstraction. Among the means of communication, we should distinguish between primary processes and secondary techniques.

221 Primary Processes

Social suggestion, gesture and language are three outstanding primary processes of communication.

2211 SOCIAL SUGGESTION

Imitation is the dominant act which secures conformity and consolidates society. Imitation is the process often involuntary, of falling in with the ways of the other members of society. In this process one picks up the ideas prevalent in society. It virtually amounts to overt communication from society to the individual. When the individual learns to go to the temple or to the library, for instance, because others do so, it is as if a communication has been received. When I went to the Birmingham Railway Station in 1924, I rushed to the booking window since I did not find anybody standing in my line of approach. But having reached the window, I glanced round. I found a long queue standing in the form of a quadrant of a circle. Nobody spoke to me or even made a gesture. And yet I felt a social suggestion. I picked it up as a communicaion and I retraced my steps and took my rightful place in the queue. Social suggestion consists of unformulated, unsymbolised, unverbalised communications of society. It is very important. One who is not familiar with such communications may be baffled by the significance of certain kinds of behaviour even if one is aware of their external forms and the verbal symbols accompanying them.

2212 GESTURE

Gesture includes manipulation of the visible and movable organs of one's body--hands, head, lips, eyebrows, eyes, etc. Variation in intonation too may have to be classed with gestures. But it must be given a place in language also. The shrugging of shoulders, the wave of hand, the clenched fist, the biting of lips, the lifting of the eye-brows and the widening of the eyes are means of communication. The silent shade-plays of yore and the modern silent movies make communication depend solely on gestures. The *Kathakalli* of Kerala uses gestures as a means for communicating a whole story. At an evening party at Kollengode, the artist communicated by gestures the substance of my speech on 'Public library provision.' His communication was even more effective than my verbal communication. Many secret societies have developed elaborate gesture-languages as they are called. Rama, the hero in Valmiki's *Ramayana*, is often described as an adept in picking up communication from mere gestures. The poet praises the hero quite often for this adeptness of his. He is also described as an expert in communicating his own ideas by subtle gestures. The other characters in the poem often betray their obtuseness in their lack of awareness and subtlety in picking up such communications from Rama. Valmiki uses this device to produce many humorous situations—extremely subtle, humour.

2213 LANGUAGE

Language is the most direct means of communication so far evolved. It had taken shape in prehistoric times. Language is the whole body of words and methods of combination of words used by a nation, people or race. It has the fullest known apparatus designed for communication. The apparatus consists of phonetic symbols which can denote every known social referent including data of sense-perception, abstractions of varying degrees made by intellect and even the speakable referents seized by intuition unmediated by senses or intellect. The referential apparatus of the language of even a primitive group is characterised by certitude, completeness to cover the ideas of the society and potentiality to accommodate any new idea which may be created by the society. The richness of its overtones is almost endless although it is only a select few that are able to harness them for effective communication. It helps creative thinking.

2214 ECLECTICISM

The most effective communication is eclectic. It combines all the above means in due proportion. With the unspoken social suggestion as background, words are uttered and their efficiency is enhanced by gestures. All the subtler effect of factors like local context, modulation of voice, change in facial expression, movement of the eyes, etc.— in short the entire interaction of the personalities of those who are communicating with one another are pressed into service. This is most effective when there are only two persons in the picture and they are intimate in their relation. In Sanskrit the term *Samvada* is reserved to denote communication *par excellence* in such a setting. The *Samvada* form of communication is usually invoked only for profound purposes like Initiations. Vedic literature emphasises this by saying that communication is a necessary link by which knowledge gets created. Indeed the teacher is called the pre-form of knowledge ; the student is called its post-form ; knowledge itself is said to emerge from their meeting ; and communication is described as the means by which it is helped to emerge.

222 Secondary Techniques

No primary process of communication is possible when space and/or time separate the two parties of a communication. To meet this situation, several secondary techniques are being invented. Writing was the first of such techniques. It had been invented even in prehistoric times. Writing makes communication possible across space and time. It makes language-transfer possible. In reality, writing uses symbolism of a kind for the purpose. The telegraph codes are other forms of symbolism of similar kind. These symbolisms can effect language-transfer exactly and without any mutilation.

In certain classes of symbolism designed for communication a literal reproduction of the original may not be possible. Wigwagging, railroad signals and temple bells belong to this category. This class of symbolism is used only when simple responses like yes or no or a simple action or abstention from action is needed and language-transfer cannot be made.

To reduce the time of communication by language-transfer several technological devices are being invented. To-day with the aid of radio waves, the radius of almost instantaneous language-transfer has been extended to cover the whole earth. Thus so far as the technology of communication is concerned, the entire surface of the earth has been virtually made fit to become a single territorial unit for co-operative living. The secondary techniques involved in these devices for communication make Delhi nearer to London than perhaps to an adjoining village. Five minutes after the Reuter's agent interviewed me in London my words were put into types by several Newspaper Offices in India. But these secondary techniques cannot by themselves effect communication. They can effect it only if the primary process *par excellence* the expression of the idea in language has been completed at one end of the communication. They cannot transfer thought *qua* thought. They can only effect language-transfer. The communication will be consumed only if the language transferred is intelligible at the other end. This condition must be fulfilled for the consummation of communication whether the aid of secondary techniques are invoked or not. Even if the two parties are face to face, communication is negatived if the second party does not know the language used by the first party. In other words, language is of the very essence of communication.

223 Babel of Tongues

There is a difficulty in this matter. It is caused by the multiplicity of languages which got developed during the past when physiographical barriers could not be got over and intermingling of people, separated by such barriers or even by sheer distance, was not common. The babel of tongues which baffles the world today is an inheritance which cannot be easily liquidated. There are said to be nearly 5,000 languages in use. It is true that all these languages are not equally influential. But the number of influential languages has been steadily increasing in the present century. Till the First World War most of the creative thought of the world was communicated through less than half a dozen languages belonging to the Teutonic and Latin groups. It is the countries, whose people speak these languages, which were dominant in the political sphere. But after the First World War the Slavonic languages got revived. The present day,—*i.e.*, the period after the Second World War, is witnessing the revival of many of the Asian languages. The simmering of Asian renaissance is unmistakable. It is true that during the last 500 years many of the Asian people had been lying in a state of exhaustion and stupor. Their languages had not been used for creative thinking or for the communication of creative thought. The result has been that these languages were paralysed. But it is not merely political motives but the irrepressible blossoming of the minds of these people who are awakening, which is going to swell the number of influential languages to beyond a dozen.

224 Attempts at Liquidation

During the last two centuries several attempts have been made to liquidate the babel of tongues. A systematic and comparative study of the attendant circumstances, agencies employed, resistances offered and the degree of success attained in these attempts should be undertaken. The results of that study may lead to a formulation of the context in which the number of languages can be reduced with profit and without any harm to anybody.

2241 REDUCTION TO ONE LANGUAGE

A comparatively small-scale sociological experiment is in progress in the U. S. A. It Americanises as the term goes. One element of Americanisation is making every citizen use English—rather American —as the medium for thinking and communication. That the U. S. A. is able to succeed in this process is due to chance. Other areas colonised by the Europeans, like Canada and South Africa, have not succeeded in this process. Having had a favourable start in the nineteenth century and having now begun to control immigration, U. S. A. succeeds in the process. A situation has arisen when everybody who seeks American citizenship has to accept the dictation that he must use American as his medium. It is the smallness of the annual driblet of immigrants which the quota system allows from any one linguistic group, which disarms them from asserting their own language. The immigrant family takes a few generations to throw off the mother-tongue and bring American to the same level as the original mother-tongue.

2242 POSSIBLE DANGER

This should involve considerable loss of creative ability in thinking. No attempt has been made to assess this loss. In assessing it, we should remember that it happens that some of the best brains in the world have sought refuge in U. S. A. during the last fifteen years. These exceptional men can easily digest a foreign language and be at home in it without loss of creative power. My conjecture is that a change over in mother-tongue will inhibit creative thinking in ordinary folk for four or five centuries.

Ballard agrees with this view. For he writes in his *Thought and Language* (1934):

"How fares the child who is bilingual from the first? An investigation carried out in Wales a few years ago caused much perturbation because it seemed to indicate that to learn two languages concurrently in early childhood retards mental development.

"Thought and inner speech are so closely interwoven that they grow and decay together. Hence we cannot cultivate the one without cultivating the other. And training in the use of the mother-tongue—the tongue in which a child thinks and dreams—becomes the first essential of schooling and the first instrument of culture."

2243 IMPRACTICABILITY

The success of the American experiment does not warrant that it will ever be practicable to reduce all the people of the world to one particular language. In the first place the peculiarly favourable conditions which obtained in the U. S. A. do not exist in the world as a whole. It is one thing to force a new tongue on immigrants who seek to enter a country in helplessness and despair, but it is another thing to force a new tongue on a settled people living in their own homeland. The British experiment in India of making English the medium of instruction, for government business and for trade, continued for more than a century, and has demonstrated the futility of attemtping to force an alien tongue on settled people of any considerable size. It is true that in about 150 years, about 5 per cent. of the population have with success adopted English as medium for thinking and communication. But to penetrate into the intellectual strata lower than the very top-most has proved almost impossible. The havoc of change over to an alien medium has been far-reaching even among the top-intellectuals of India. It is commonly remarked that there has been very little creative work in India during the last 100 years, though it had not been lacking in brilliant brains. It needs examination how far this is traceable to the intellectually upper-most centiles having begun to learn and think through and in a foreign tongue. For as H. R. Huss says in *Illiteracy of the literate* " Men who can speak a number of different tongues are notorious for having little to say anything of them."

2244 RESISTANCE

There is evidence of forcing a foreign language in the colonies in Africa. A few Africans, whom I had met, are not happy about this. They resent it. The African languages which are sought to be replaced in this manner are not rich in their past literature. The conditions are, therefore, more favourable to wipe out indigenous languages in these colonies than in India. I am told that the absence of a script is another factor which may prove favourable to this experiment. It is too early to say whether the experiment will succeed.

2245 IMPOVERISHMENT OF HUMANITY

In the *Winged destiny*, Fiana Macleod protests against the suppression of the mother tongue with great feeling. She writes:

"The last tragedy for broken nations is not the loss of power and distinction, nor even the loss of that independence which is so vital to the commonwealth. It is not perhaps even the loss of the country, though there is no harder thing than to see the smoke of the stranger, or to hear upon the wind the forlorn business of the going of those who are dispossessed and the coming of those new in possession. The last tragedy, and the saddest, is when the treasured language dies slowly out . . . . The whole tendency in our modern days is for the stronger nations, such as Britain, France and the United States, to overwhelm the weaker, to annihilate their culture, to swamp their language. This makes not for the enrichment but for the impoverishment of humanity. Losing its native speech, a people loses its continuity with the past and sinks to intellectual helotry."

2246 HERITAGE

The babel of tongues should be examined from the angle of human heritage, in order to understand why its liquidation would be impracticable and what can be done in the circumstances. At first sight it looks as if a common language for international communication should be possible. For there are certain primordially common elements in all languages. These are the result of the existence of a fundamental common nature in human beings. For example, the physiological organs of speech are in essential points formed alike in all races. The anatomical differences, say in the arching of the palate or in the size and form of the nasal chamber, are not sufficient to make a fundamenal difference in linguistic development. This means the system of articulate sound is virtually the same and that changes in it are also the same in all languages. For example single consonants between vowels tend to become voiced in all languages. A stress accent often has the effect of obscuring the vowels in weak syllables in all languages. Psychologically too much is commn to all man kind. This means that there has been as much probability for common semantics to have evolved as for common phonetics. However, there have been adverse factors too. Man is only in part a reasonable being. Many of human developments are therefore unpredictable, irrational and illogical. Further the earlier days isolated groups of human beings caught up in physiographical pockets, with hardly any contact or frequent communication between one another. In naming an object or an experience it was a characteristic which was striking at the chance-moment when it was named, that decided the name. These two factors had led to considerable semantic difference. The convenience of sticking to the name first hit upon even after it ceased to be truly descriptive led to emphasise the difference between the word-stock of different groups. This was possible because what had to be represented in the word was the minimum quality by which one would be able to recognise what it denoted. Just as in order to recognise a person we do not need to see the whole man, so in the world of languages it is often enough to get a bare hint. Often we need no more than the way in which a friend knocks at the door to recognise him. These factors made different groups develop their languages along diverse lines even if they had started together. Thus long before the population of the world increased and the distributions of the density of population on the one hand and the density of consumable commodities on the other ceased to register with each other on the face of the earth, several languages had established themselves and formed essential parts of the heritage of the respective groups. These languages have already become so immiscible and so deeply ingrained in the nature of those who speak them naturally that it is next to impossible to reduce them to a single language. Within the last 1,000 years at least a dozen of the current Indian languages had been formed by these factors, and they are now irremovable parts of the heritage of the respective people. The demand for the re-drawing of the boundaries of the constituent States of India on a linguistic basis is inexorable. At best it can be delayed. It can never be prevented.

225 Prevention of Dispersal

This does not mean that this process of adding to the babel of tongues will go on for ever or should be allowed to go on for ever. For several natural and social factors have come into the picture during the last two or three centuries, which may prevent further dispersal.

2251 NATURAL RETARDATION

In the first place the pressure of population and industrialisation have made the pattern of distribution of populaton on the earth put itself away from the pattern of distribution of the natural resources needed for the maintenance of life. This calls for an inter-mingling of the people within any nation. This retards the formation of dialects and their movement towards interdependence.

2252 INTER-PENETRATING TRANSPORT

Another factor which arrests the further formation of independent languages is due to the increasingly intensive mutual intercourse between different sections of a linguistic group living in different territories. This intercourse is the result of the strides which technology is making in the development of communication and transport of persons. Even though the 150 millions who speak English are scattered in all the five continents, there is little appreciable dispersal of English into independent languages. It has been mentioned that in 1820 when transport facilities were meagre, tnere was only one family who spoke standard French in Sotbillier (Berne). All the other families spoke the local dialect. But by 1896 there were only a few old people left to talk the local dialect. This was due to the intermingling of people brought about by transport facilities. As a contrast mention may be made of the fact that every single village on the Macley Coast in the north-east of New Guinea has its own dialect. Villages six or eight miles apart can hardly understand each other. Even so tiny an islet as Thru Hills, which is but six miles long, has two distinct linguistic groups which do not understand each other. All this will disappear as soon as inter-penetration of transport mixes these people together.

2253 POLITICAL UNIFICATION

Another factor which usually thwarts the aspiration of dialects to the status of independent languages is political unification or alliance. The United Kingdom is a prominent example of this. The last five centuries have seen how the different dialects of English even those like Scotch and Welsh which belonged to other subfamilies and had already attained near-independent status—have abstained from claiming separate existence. It is hoped that the political unification of India will prevent the further multiplication of languages in India. In particular it may be expected that the tendency of Hindi to break into two or three independent languages will be arrested.

2254 LITERACY AND LITERATURE

During the last 100 years a new force is taking shape in the developed countries to counter-act the tendency to dispersal. Literacy has become nearly universal. Reading materials are being produced in plenty to suit all intellectual levels and interests. A network of free libraries has been established. Popular periodicals and newspapers are produced in plenty and circulated everywhere. The same printed word impinges on the mind of everybody. This counteracts the spontaneous dispersal of a language in course of time.

2255 STANDARD LANGUAGE

The emergence of 'Standard' language—Standard English, Standard French, etc.,—is driving out the dialects caused by physiographical factors. Standard language is of social determination. Many factors contribute to this formation—marriage, religion, community, school, literature and so on. Nowadays the broadcast talks which reach practically every home has begun to wield a great influence in this matter. Universities and Schools contribute a good deal towards the maintenance of standard language. The system of periodical transfer of officials helps the survival and spread of the standard language. Of course transport facilities are increasing the radius of reach of standard language. People realise that the standard language opens the door to understanding in wider circles than does a dialect, whether it is speech or writing. The respect for standard English is likely to prolong and perhaps make permanent the homogeneity of language among the 150 millions of people who speak English today though they are scattered all over the earth. In India it is hoped that standard Hindi will emerge much more quickly than it had been possible for the languages which established their standards in the earliest centuries. If it does, it will be an effeetive binding force which will prevent dispersal.

226 Preservation of Homogeneity

Apart from factors which prevent the breaking up of an existing language into several languages, there are also certain social techniques which are being used to preserve the homogeneity of a linguistic group. The experiment in progress in the United States on a national scale has already been mentioned in Section 2241. There immigrants from other linguistic groups are by law and social pressure oblig-ed to adopt the language of the nation. In a polyglot country which gets politically unified a similar techinique may be adopted. It has to be assumed that commonsense will prevail and that the constituent States will be made linguistically homogeneous. On this assumption it should be possible for a constituent State to make it obligatory for the residents of other linguistic states to learn the language of the State of adoption if they wish to change their residence. The *Constitution of India* needs to be examined from this point of view. Articles, 19, 29 and 30 in Part 3 Fundamental Rights may, on the surface, appear to be against such a step being taken by any constituent State. For section 29 (1) and (2) reads:

"(1) Any section of the citizens residing in the territory of India or any part thereof having a distinct language, script or culture of its own, shall have the right to conserve the same.

(2) No citizen shall be denied admission into any educational institution maintained by the State or receiving aid out of State funds on grounds only of religion, race, caste, language or any of them."

Can these articles be construed to disable a constituent State from enforcing citizens coming from other lingusitic areas to adopt the. language of itself? It may not be necessary to enforce it by positive action but it will amount to enforcing if schools and libraries adopt only the language in the State as the medium. Article 19 (1) which reads:

"All citizens shall have the right—

"(*d*) to move freely throughout the territory of India;

(*e*) to reside and settle in any part of the territory of India."

will also have the same effect as Article 29.

Article 30 (2) might militate against the exercise of this right by a constituent State. For it reads:

"(1) All minorities, whether based on religion or language, shall have the right to establish and administer educational institutions of their choice.

(2) The State shall not, in granting aid to educational institutions, discriminate against any educational institution on the ground that it is under the management of a minority, whether based on religion or language."

In the long run provision of Article 30 has the potentiality to break up the linguistic homegeneity of a constituent State in due course. Evidently, this article was framed in view of the present heterogeneously-linguistic constituent States and particularly of metropolitan cities like Bombay, Calcutta, Delhi and Madras. Whatever be the legal loophole, there is no doubt that social pressure will preserve the linguistic homogeneity of each state.

227 Voluntary Bi-lingualism

To maintain a language it requires a certain minimum of population. The minimum is high in modern days where people depend so much on printed books and newspapers. Printing trade cannot flourish unless there is an adequate market. It is so with the Daily Press also. Again the creative thinkers in a community will find it difficult to find a sufficient number of peers for mutual intercourse within the community itself unless it has a minimum population. No scientific study has been made to determine what the minimum should be for these two purposes. The history of the linguistic curriculum of the schools in Scandinavian countries throws some light on what I call 'Voluntary bi-lingualism.' Before they were developed, at some time the Scandinavian was spoken by one-million people. Later it split into Danish spoken by three millions, Norwegian spoken by three millions and Swedish spoken by six millions and two other languages. However, during the last 50 years as these countries began to develop and became more aware of the conditions requisite for healthy progress, they found it unwise for small nations to insulate themselves within one language. First they attempted to take German as the second language. In recent years they have made English a compulsory second language in all educational institutions. The regulation provides for it and the people welcome it. While travelling through these countries, I found that there was no resistance whatever to this bi-lingualism. There was every evidence that it was voluntary. The Scandinavians even produce books in English language. In international meetings they do have an advantage over other nations which confine themselves to a single language.

228 Conclusion

We have been reduced to a dilemma. International peace is possible only if the terrestrial unit of co-operative living covers the whole earth, that is if a World-State becomes a reality. For this to happen and to continue without reversion, understanding should be possible and easy among the entire humanity, across the entire surface of the earth. Understanding is possible only if communication is possible. Communication across the earth's space is possible and easy only if the primary process of communication is through the medium of a single language. While forces have taken shape to prevent the formation of new languages, the immiscible languages are already too many in number and too varied in their nature to allow of the liquidation of the babel of tongues or to reduce them even to two or three. With the result, we must recognise the existence of several unextinguishable languages and explore how best international understanding can be facilitated. One possible approach is to devise different aids to communication in different spheres of international intercourse and co-operative living. Accordingly Commerce, Political relation, Literature, and Intellectual pursuit will be examined from the point of view of communication. The opportunity which classificatory language will find to facilitate international communication will be explored in particular.

CHAPTER 23

Commercial Contact

So far as commercial contact is concerned, the babel of tongues was not a serious handicap in the past. For in commerce, the physical presence of the commodity and the currency goes a long way in facilitating communication. A smattering of commercial terms and of tourist vocabulary will prove to be a sufficient medium for communication. Chinamen do trade in India to-day without either their knowing Indian languages or our knowing Chinese. I had met Indian traders doing very well in England without any proficiency in English.

231 Early Period

This had been sufficient for centuries. The people of the Gujarat Coast of India had been trading with the people of the East Coast of Africa for several centuries with great success and without any need for reduction to a single language or for attaining scholarship in each other's language. Within India itself, we find Kabulis trading in South India and Tamils doing business in North India without either attaining any proficiency in the language of the locality or giving up their own mother tongue. Till the mariner's compass was brought into wide use in the fourteenth century, the quantity of trade was very small and it was only between adjoining countries. The number of persons employed in commerce was therefore very small and the number of languages encountered by them was seldom more than one or two. Trade was mostly by barter in those far-off days. No difficulty was, therefore, experienced in making communication serve the needs of commercial contact without the necessity for a considerable knowledge of languages or reduction in the number of languages.

232 Period of Sailing Ships

When sailing ships guided by mariner's compass began to cross high seas, trade began to connect distant countries. The languages of such countries were far too unfamiliar and unlike. The traders were obliged to spend long periods amidst a foreign language. But even then, the difficulties of medium were reduced to a minimum by each group of traders specialising in one country, so that commercial contact was often bilateral. Interpreters grew up as a profession. In spite of a certain percentage of trouble arising out of intentional or unintentional wrong interpretation, communication went on all right. It was mostly oral and seldom written. The dangers of a babel of tongues did not take serious shape.

233 Modern Times

However, in modern times large scale world-wide competitive commerce has set in. It is being regulated and controlled at governmental level. It gets entangled in a maze of foreign exchange and commercial intercourse. The personnel employed in commercial transactions fall into three groups. The quality of the intercourse differs in these groups. The difficulties of communication are differently incident on these groups and different solutions may be possible.

234 Carriers

The first group consists only of carriers *qua* carriers. The region of ideas in which they have to communicate with people speaking other languages is both definite and limited. The personnel of this group also is very specialised. It is not difficult for these personnel to acquire efficiency in the jargon of their calling, which prevails in different linguistic areas. In their case, therefore, the babel of tongues does not create any major problem in communication.

235 Clearance and Customs Staff

The second group involving international commerce consists of the staff in charge of clearance work and customs. Here there is greater complication. One reason for complication is the enormous increase, in modern times, in the range of commodities figuring in commerce. It is no longer merely raw materials or near-raw materials, which are comparatively limited in number. But the commodities of commerce include myriads of manufactured and semi-manufactured materials and even artificial materials. The increase in their number is further multiplied by the increase in the number of their grades and brands. The terminology used to denote this vast range of materials is not standardised even in the natural lanuages of the regions where they are produced or consumed. The difficulties faced in communication by the babel of tongues, therefore, get even more pronounced. To minimise these difficulties internanational organisations have attempted to make standard lists of commodities with names in several languages. The *Draft customs nomenclature* (1931) by the Sub-committee of Experts for the Unification of Customs Tariff Nomenclature of the Economic Committee of the League of Nations. (Series of League of Nations publications, II Economic and financial, 1931, II B 25). (League of Nations, C 921. M486, 1931, II B) is an example of this kind. The alphabetical arrangement which is resorted to at present is not helpful to communication as it ruthlessly scatters commodites which are closely akin to one another or which generally figure together in commerce. Moreover the commodities are thrown in different orders in the alphabetical lists of the different languages. The broad grouping given in the League of Nations publication is not as helpful as necessary.

2351 CLASSIFICATORY LANGUAGES

It occurs to me that classification may be able to give some relief in the difficulties of communication in this matter. Probably it can also reduce the cost of maintaining such standard lists and keeping them ever hospitable to accommodate new commodites in a helpful manner. But there are difficulties. Commodities are by definition the most concrete materials one can think of. In other words, their extension is least. They are also many in number. They were estimated to exceed one million, even in 1927. The result is that natural languages give up attempting to give them expressive or descriptive names. Most of the commodities are given only pure extensional names that is, mere denotative names with little descriptive or expressive elements in them. Classificatory language, which by its very definition should be expressive, will therefore be put to great strain in constructing class numbers for commodities. Here parsimony in length of class number and expressiveness will come into acute conflict. But it is my hope that the foundations of expressive analytico-synthetic classification can be explored and properly laid so as to resolve this conflict and establish classificatory language as a universal artificial auxiliary language fit to be a helpful medium of communication in clearance and customs work. As its use will be confined to a closed circle of specialists, it will not get shattered and mangled as the natural languages which have to grow in the mouth of the man in the street.

236 Commercial Houses

The third group of personnel playing an essential part in modern global commerce consists of those who work behind desks in the commercial houses in the different countries. They do not have the benefit of the physical presence of the commodity to help in their communication with one another. Nor do they have the immediate presence of the other party. Communication has therefore to be only by language-transfer. Moreover they have to negotiate by correspondence on diverse matters including the fixing of price, assessing demand and supply, export and import control, foreign exchange, entering into contract and so on. Their work marks the transitioning of commercial contact into political understanding. The problems of communication among these groups are not therefore different from those arising among those who communicate with one another for political understanding. The bad effect of having too many languages and the possible methods of minimising it need not therefore be separately examined here.

CHAPTER 24

Political Understanding

The greatest resistance to the extension of the territorial limit of co-operative living to the entire area of the earth is met with at the political level. It is here that the devil in man has the greatest sway. The devil manipulates the passion and the ego in a ruthless manner. It often takes the form of fear. It seeks to perpetuate faults in communication. It thrives on equivocation and communication with mental reservation. It revels in the existence of a babel of tongues. Communication for political understanding has not got the chance to directness nor the help of concreteness of context as commercial contact has. Humanity has been, however, endeavouring to escape from the ruinous hold of the devil by providing better modes of communication. In the past, it has been able to bring the devilish passion and egotism under control among a linguistically homogeneous people. In this process, it has learnt that communication plays a great part. By a free communication of ideas, people in monolinguistic nations have succeeded in demarcating the spheres of loyalty to the nation and to smaller groups within it. This has encouraged humanity to help better communication at the international level and to attempt to demarcate the sphere of international co-operative living and that of the constituent nations. But heterogeneity of language is sought to be met for the first time on a publicly organised basis. The heterogeneity is more pronounced when we take the world as a whole than when we consider a polyglot country like India or Russia. The languages in India virtually belong to the same family. They are near-cousins. Most of them got separated from their common ancestor and assumed autonomy only during the last 1,000 years or so. But the languages in the world-forum belong to totally different families. They had grown in totally different social atmospheres. They have become immisicible. They differ as widely as one can imagine in their alphabet, even in the direction in which letters and words are written—left to right, right to left, top to bottom and so on—in their radicals, their morphological and syntactical methods and their semantic characteristics. There is little common ground. This creates a colossal problem which faces international communication. In spite of it, Herculean attempts are being made to aid the language by bringing it towards the level of *Samvada* (*vide* section 2214) in which all the other primary processes of communication mentioned in Chapter 2 can be pressed into service. International conference is the resulting forum. Here political differences are sought to be ironed out with a view to establishing a World-State. We shall examine how the difficulties due to multiplicity of languages is being sought to be overcome.

241 A Single Language

In the past attempts have been made to make communication easy by the adoption of a single language as the official language of a conference. In Europe, Latin was so adopted for centuries. But by the turn of the present century, Latin proved to be too strange and burdensome. French slipped into its place. It was unchallenged till the First World War.

242 Two Languages

But the Paris Peace Conference bracketed French and English as of equal status. The League of Nations inherited this parity and Rule 16 of the Rules of Procedure of its Assembly provided:

"1. Speeches in French shall be summarised in English, and *vice versa*, by an interpreter belonging to the Secretariat.

"2. A representative speaking in another language shall provide for the translation of his speech into one of these two languages.

"3. All documents, resolutions and reports circulated by the President or the Secretariat shall be rendered in both French and English."

But in a few years, English began to slip down, as the following table of percentages of speeches in French and English, made at the General Assembly, shows:

	1920 Per cent.	1927 Per cent.
French	65	77
English	35	22
German		1

Spanish, Portuguese, German and other languages have been persistently endeavouring to get recognised as additional official languages. The International Labour Organisation was the first to accept Spanish as a third official language. The addition of each extra language means addition to the conference-time and the cost of communication. The addition to conference-time is minimised by taking help from technology for simultaneous translation. This was first put to large scale use at the 17th International Geological Congress in Moscow in 1937.

After the Second World War, English is becoming dominant. In 1943, the United Nations Food and Agricultural Conference adopted English as the official language in spite of the protest of the French representative. So it was with the United Nations Relief and RehabilitationA dministration (1943) and Monetary and Financial Conference (1944).

243 More Languages

The Rules of Procedure of the General Assembly of the United Nations, as adopted on 17 November, 1947, at Flushing Meadows provide for five Official Languages, three of which are singled out as Working Languages. The choice of the languages had been conditioned by the then international situation. It may have to be altered as the international situation changes. Here are the relevant Rules of Procedure:

VIII Languages

Rule 44. Chinese, English, French, Russian and Spanish shall be the official languages of the General Assembly, its committees and sub-committees. English, French and Spanish shall be the working languages.

Rule 45. Speeches made in any of the working languages shall be interpreted into the other two working languages.

Rule 46. Speeches made in either of the other two official languages shall be interpreted into the three working languages.

Rule 47. Any representative may make a speech in a language other than the official languages. In this case, he shall himself provide for interpretation into one of the working languages. Interpretation into the other working languages by the interpreters of the Secretariat may be based on the interpretation given in the first working language.

Rule 48. Verbatim records shall be drawn up in the working languages. A translation of the whole or part of any verbatim record into either of the two official languages shall be furnished if requested by any delegation.

Rule 49. Summary records shall be drawn up as soon as possible in the official languages.

Rule 50. The Journal of the General Assembly shall be issued in the working languages.

Rule 51. All resolutions and other important documents shall be made available in the official languages. Upon the request of any representative, any other document shall be made available in any or all of the official languages.

Rule 52. Documents of the General Assembly, its committees and sub-committees, shall, if the General Assembly so decides, be published in any languages other than the official languages."

244 Grounds of Claim

The claim of the different languages for a place in the Babel of Tongues is not always based on necessity or convenience. It is often based on considerations of prestige and political importance. Adoption of many official languages lands one in enormous waste of time in effecting communication.

Adoption of one language lands in failure of communication. There is also the dog-fight over the choice of the single official language. In fact the choice is best done by casting lots. One language will prove as good as any other. All languages grow by usage. Use as the official language for international communication will soon make it as good a medium as any other. There is nothing permanent in the attributes of languages painted in the following statement of the Russian author Lomonosov who wrote two centuries ago : " Charles V, King of Spain and Roman Emperor, used to say that with God it is best to speak Spanish ; French with friends ; German to an enemy ; and with women, Italian. Had he known the Russian language also, he might have concluded that it is propitious always to speak Russian with everyone. For in the Russian, he would have found the majesty of Spanish, the vivacity of French, the vigour of German, the tenderness of Italian, and beyond all this, the richness and strength of precise description of Greek and Latin." Every language can make this claim. Even the least developed language current among primitive people and certainly every one of the once-developed and recently paralysed Indian languages can say " Give me the opportunity and I shall rise to the occasion."

Language of the Smallest Group

A deliberate choice of the language of any one nation for the monopoly of being used for international communication would meet with insurmountable difficulties on account of international jealousies. Also it would put that nation at an advantage over others. As jealousy becomes as explosive as a dynamite only between large and influential nations or between linguistic groups of vast proportion, visionaries had proposed the languages of the smaller nations for the privilege of the monopoly, say—Norwegian or Armenian! In the first place, it would require superhuman effort to make people all over the world take up the study of a language current only among two or three millions. Secondly, it would be a doubtful boon to the nation thus promoted to the most-favoured position; for it will have to see its beloved tongue mutilated and trampled under foot everywhere.

246 Artificial Auxiliary Language

Can political understanding be better promoted by the use of an artificial language as official language? Some have thought that the adoption of such an artificial auxiliary language equally foreign to every nation can be a solution. It may be so on grounds of political considerations or of equity. But it will, in reality, amount to making all the nations 'have-nots,' because we cannot make all of them equally 'haves.' On strictly practical grounds this is unacceptable. Is the artificial language to be used as medium for thinking by those who habitually attend international conferences? If so, will not this language too develop varying over tones in the mouths of different people? Will it not very soon become not fully understood by all alike? At the other extreme, if it does not yield to be so changed by the speakers by variation of overtones, it may be too sterile to be used for the intimate and heart-to-heart communication which international political conferences are expected to provide for. Moreover the history of the dozen artificial languages, which have been constructed during the last fifty years, shows that they are not altogether impartial to all the natural languages. They are often drawing far more from one natural language than from others. This means that they are subject to most of the objections which are raised against a natural language.

2461 CLASSIFICATORY LANGUAGE

It is doubtful if classificatory language can ever be carried to the stage of being fit for debate on political problems and relations. A debate needs all parts of speech. But a classificatory language contains only substantives and conjunctions. As its distinctive function is to arrange and mechanise arrangement, it cannot take up other parts of speech without ceasing to be classificatory language.

247 Conclusion

The difficulties of the promotion of international understanding by communication through a single language, natural or artificial, appear to be insoluble at present. It is at the political level that national passion and egotism are least amenable to control. Words have to be used with greater effect and precision for certain purposes. They have also to make the deepest emotional appeal for certain other purposes. Artificial languages may not lend themselves to this double purpose. It is not enough in the political arena if the general gist is picked up. Every word must be understood and every overtone should be detected and assessed. Even translations into another natural language proves inadequate for this double purpose. The overtones will totally flout artificial languages. Perhaps the only solution will be to recognise one of the widely used natural languages as the only working language. India proposes to solve a similar difficulty by singling out Hindi as the official language on the ground that it is the language which is spoken by the largest group in India. Those whose mother-tongue is not Hindi are at a disadvantage. And yet there appears to be no other solution to preserve India as a whole as a territorial unit for co-operative living. So it is if a World-State is to become a reality and if the territorial unit for co-operative living is to cover the entire earth.

CHAPTER 25

Literary Exchange

The service of classificatory language to communication in the primary process of language is even more doubtful in the case of literary exchange than in the case of political understanding. It is doubtful not only in communication between different linguistic groups but also within one and the same linguistic group. For the over-tones are even more numerous in literary expressions than in political utterances. Richness of over-tone is indeed a measure of the profoundness of a piece of literature.

251 Suggestion

Mahamahopadhyaya Professor S. Kuppuswami Sastriar used to emphasise that a Sanskrit school of literary criticism was called the 'School of Over-tones.' According to this school, literature leans more upon suppression than on expression. This means that the actual endeavour of a literary artist should be no more than to throw forth suggestions. Goethe claims that it can be no more than a suggestion. He states this on the basis of his own experience as a poet. He says that when a poet dives into his own depths, picks out his poetic experience, and recedes from the depths towards the level of consciousness, he finds that only a divine language can express his experience. But no such language is available. Even if it were, it cannot communicate anything to the common men. He is therefore obliged to use the language current in his community. He irradiates it so profoundly that its glow is extremely rich in colour. Each member of the audience picks up only that colour which the lens of his own experience permits to pass through. His lens may perhaps allow the slipping through of only a wee-bit of the other colour in the immediate proximity to what is specific to himself. All the other colours will certainly be screened off. It is usually the filtering in of this extra colour which stimulates him or gives him solace. He is blind to all the other colours. This implies that the primary process of natural language fails to be a fully transparent medium for communication. The difference between what is originated at the source and what is received at the other end is considerable. The medium of language is not totally expressive.

252 Everlasting Quarry

However, to change the figure of speech, what the literary artist intended to communicate lies stratified in innumerable beds in his work. It is open to the man at the other end to come back and quarry what is imbedded at deeper levels as and when he acquires fresh experience that can be used as sharper tools to extract from the quarry. The experience with our premier poem Valmiki's *Ramayana* is just this in the case of most readers. During the last 35 years I have gone through 30 cycles of re-reading it. Surely my stock of experience and my apperceptive mass had been necessarily enlarged during this long stretch of years. They have been added to gradually year after year. The result has been that in each cycle of reading, the same old words of Valmiki communicated to me progressively varying streams of thought. By definition a classificatory language should have one-to-one correspondence with the thought represented by it. It should admit of no stratification in meaning. It must yield its meaning in its entirety in one instalment. It is therefore totally unsuited to serve in the communication of the transcendental experience of a literary artist.

253 Beauty of Form

It has been said that what distinguishes literature from ordinary writing is its beauty of form, its rhythm, in short its aesthetic appeal. In other words literature is a fine art using as its medium, not marble or canvas and colour, but language. Its content is not the thought-content but something more elusive than thought. No doubt there is thought in literature and fine arts. But it occurs in them at its transition stage when it passes into that something which is more elusive. The charm of literature consists in the presentation of thought in such a phase of dissolution. But classification is a bare act of intellection and classificatory language is designed only to represent thought in its dry-as-dust phase. Classificatory laguage cannot transmit beauty of form.

254 Emotional Appeal

Another essential quality of literature is said to be its emotional appeal. It is true that the purpose why the emotions are brought in a literary communication is totally different from what is aimed at in a political harangue. In the latter it is to stir up passion, activate it and even intensify it. On the other hand the purpose of literature is to purge the audience of all lower passions and to sublimate them. It is the unexpressed suggestions in literary communication which do this task. But classificatory language is designed to be expressive of all the facets and phases involved. It cannot therefore transmit emotional appeal.

255 Aroma of personality

Another way in which a literary piece differs from ordinary writing is that it is fully charged with the personality of the author— the person who communicates. It is the authorial aroma which distinguishes literature from ordinary communication. Even in other subjects where usually thought-content alone counts—even in a subject like Mathematics—it is possible to have books charged with the personality of the author. I call them classics. The aroma of classics as well as literary writing is too elusive for classificatory language.

256 Futile Devices

Qualities such as those described above make communication incomplete even within the same language. Frantic efforts have been made to help literary communication complete its task by devices like paraphrascs glosses and commentaries. It is notorious how all these devices merely swell verbosity, achieve little, and often even misdirect and inhibit the native capacity of the audience to pick up the original communication by repeated attempts in the light of growing experience over a long range of years.

257 Futility of Translations

It is no wonder then that literary exchange between two linguistic groups is even more ineffective. The only person who can help literary exchange between two linguistic groups is the poet who can use for communication either language with equal facility and flair. Such poets I would call Bridge Poets. Rabindra Nath Tagore is a supreme example of a Bridge Poet in our own times. His equal mastery of Bengali and English made possible the communication of the genius of Bengali literature to the English speaking world and *vice versa.* It is not by translation that he achieved this. Translation can only translate verbal carcasses. The soul often escapes away in the process. Translation will always stand transcended by the problem of literary exchange whatever be the possibility of mechanising translation by the use of modern computing devices of very high speed, capacity and logical flexibility. At best, translations can only stimulate the literary artists in a foreign language.

258 Forbidden Realm

Literary exchange is thus out of bounds for classificatory language. Whether it is communication of literary creation within a linguistic group or between different linguistic groups, classification cannot be of any use. Classificationists and classifiers should not arrogate to themselves capacity to achieve anything whatever in the realm of the communication of literary creation. Though I have devoted a large part of this life-time of mine to the building up and improvement of classificatory language, I am second to none in declaring that literary exchange is a forbidden realm which classification should never enter. It must stop with individualising authors and works and never presume to classify the thought-contents.

CHAPTER 26

Spiritual Communion

There is still another level of communication far more subtle than even the literary one. It is mystical experience. Indeed literary communion is only a distant approximation to mystic communion. Mystical experience is in fact " unspeakable."

26I An Anecdote

An utterance of a great mystic, who lived in the nineteenth century and the last of whose disciples lived till recently, illustrates this point. The mystic referred to is Sri Ramakrishna, in whose name a mission has been established for promotion of spiritual awareness and social service not only in India but in several other countries. One of his disciples has recorded the following anecdote. The sage looked unusually sad one day. One nearest to him asked him why it was so. He said that he felt sad because he was not able to communicate to humanity the most precious and pre-potent part of his experience. It related to *Samadhi* which means getting into the state of Identity with the Absolute. He wished to communicate to his immediate disciples and to humanity at large the delight of *Samadhi*. He wished to remember his progression into that state of delight as he entered *Samadhi*. But it often happened that up to a point he could be conscious of the various factors and of the varying qualities of the delight but when it reached beyond a certain degree of intensity he was enveloped with the sense of Identity so completely that there was nothing to see or sense. There was nothing structural. There was no pattern which is the very essence of what calls for expression. Similarly when he receded from *Samadhi* until he got out of the threshold of supreme delight, the Identity continued to negative the structure and the pattern needed for expression. This is an experience of the same order as the one described by Goethe.

262 Intuition and Illumination

Persons of this order are self-centres of illumination. Their experience is unmediated by the primary senses or the intellect. It is direct experience of the thing-in-itself. The faculty by which they do so may be called intuition. The term used in Sanskrit tradition to denote this faculty is *Divya chakshus* which may be verbally translated as divine insight. The climax in the *Bhagvad gita* is Krishna endowing Arjuna with that faculty to see globally all things-in-themselves. The *Ramayana* also refers to this all comprehensive unmediated intuition and experience and uses the word *Tapas* to denote the means by which intuition is developed.

263 True Realism

If we accept mystic experience, we shall also have to accept two types of realism. Some distinguish them as the atomic and the organic. Vedic tradition distinguishes them as *Kartr Tantra* (action-dependent) and *Vastu Tantra* (thing-dependent). *Kartr Tantra* realism tends to view the universe as made of distinct, separate or separable entities, things or concepts. Arguments and communication have to rest on sharp alternatives. Their roots are in the soil of atomism. In *Vastu Tantra* realism there are no sharp antithesis and distinction. It has its roots in the view which regards all *Kartr Tantra* reality as the creature of truncated context and is therefore in the true sense incomplete. According to it, it is only the whole universe which can be the real subject of significant communication. It tends to avoid superficial clarity and simplicity. It calls attention to the unspeakable complexity of experience. It systematically undervalues the importance of abstraction.

264 Beyond Bounds

This distinction between intellection and intuition—rationalistic and mystic experience—decides the fate of classificatory language in the realm of mystic experience. The function of classificatory language is to help us to negotiate broad outlines, and to emphasise sharp distinctions and clear subdivisions of structure. But the distinctiveness of the mystic is being conscious of the wealth of being and experience not yet been made definite which perhaps can never be made definite. "All class numbers," he says to the classifier, "are clear and stand in ordered sequence next to one another in definite positions; but that to which they point is wider and deeper. Clearness and definiteness are dearly purchased at the price of comprehensive and deep awareness. Clarity and simplicity are merely the result of superficiality and wilfull narrowness." These words the mystic utters not only to classificatory language but to any language whatever—indeed to any form of communication that we know of.

265 The Limiting Mode of Communication

The pathetic inadequacy of the primary process of language, and still more that of classificatory language, are symbolised by the following well-known picture of Indian tradition : " What a wonder? Look into the shade of the banian tree. There is a young Master sitting at the root. He is radiant. There is communication in silence. The disciples are all old. They are irradiated. Their doubts look dissolved." Surely communication at this level cannot lean upon either natural language or classificatory language. Communication has to be through direct unmediated communion.

CHAPTER 27

Cultural Concord

In Chapter 23 we saw the material level in which communication through the primary process of language is considerably helped by the physical presence of commodities. The commodities are distinct entities in which discreteness and structure appealing to the primary senses are at their best. These very features of them make classification thoroughly compatible with the level of commercial contact and profitably applicable therein. In Chapters 25 and 26 on the other hand we saw the incompatibility between classification and the profound levels of existence in which man intuits identity with everything, with the Universe itself. In those noumenal levels there is no structure and so there is nothing to be arranged, *i.e.*, classified. In international relation, clssification becomes a necessity in commercial contact but becomes impossible in literary exchange and mystical communion. In between these two extremes we have two levels which are neither totally noumenal nor wholly atomised. These are the levels of cultural and intellectual life. In these, classification has a definite part to play.

271 Cultural Polarity

Culture is a difficult word. Its dictionary definition that it is a state of civilisation is not very helpful. Culture is an abstract word. It stands for something intangible. It is indeed a quality. It is a subtle quality not directly perceivable by the senses. It is a quality which characterises the method used by man in his pursuit of happiness. Happiness is the ultimate sought by everybody. But there appears to be something slimy in this seeking. In the present state of human evolution, it is either the defensive or offensive modes of pursuit of happiness that is dominant. But the mode that will bring lasting happiness is the peaceful mode—peace with the elements, peace with the processes, peace with the things, peace with the plants, peace with the beasts, peace with the birds and particularly peace with the humans. But as D. H. Lawrence puts it in his *Psychoanalysis and the unconscious*, woe betide us, the unspeakable agony we suffer from the failure to establish and maintain the vital circuits between ourselves and other human beings. The tortures which civilised people proceed to suffer, once they have solved for themselves the bread-and-butter problem of alimentation, will not bear thought. The whole of international life is one long, blind effort at a polarity, and the whole of modern life is a shrieking failure.

272 Aetiology

The polarity is between the status of offence and defence. Between any two groups of people and particularly between any two nations today, the mutual exchange of this status is as incessant as the physicists assume to exist between protons and neutrons. It is almost impossible to catch any one nation staying totally at one pole. This offensive *cum* defensive existence produces all kinds of tension charged with low emotions like envy and hatred. At bottom this polarity and all its ugly concomitants stem from fear of each other. The fear between two human groups is not of the same order as the one between animals of different natural groups. A good deal of fear between human groups is avoidable. A proper understanding of each other will avoid much of the fear. Communication can bring about proper understanding. When communication is cut out or is through refractory medium through a medium which is not understood or which is misunderstood—misunderstanding sets in and fear follows.

273 Diagnosis

Cultures differ at the phenomenal level. But the difference thins out as we dive deep towards the noumenal level. If the cultural activities and beliefs of different groups are sorted out and arranged according to a scheme of classification, and the corresponding categories in the several groups are put against one another and compared, the causal factors of conflict stand out sharply. These will then be seen to belong, not to essentials, but to ever-changing forms. If the classification is of the analytico-synthetic variety, its apparatus for phase-analysis and facet-analysis will do this effectively and help the diagnosis of cultural conflicts.

274 Pathology

Cultural conflict is often due to a partial view of the cultural outlook and ways of life of one another. The partial view is often the result of the nebulousness in which one lands when one is not helped by an analytico-synthetic approach which a good scheme of classification can provide. Cultural conflict arises also from inability to overlook what is common in the activities and views of different cultural groups and to dwell on the differences alone. The differences induce alienation, intolerance, hatred and strife. It is often the case that differences in the total setting of a cultural group had led to differences in social beliefs and practices. Failure to sense the differences in the setting deprives one of a sympathetic understanding of the differences in practice and so reconciling them to one another as to prevent development of tension.

275 Preventive Steps

It is through public education that cultural conflicts have to be prevented. It should be a long-term programme. The schools and the children's libraries will have to work it out. They should give up the methods of indoctrination—*i.e.*, thrusting ready-made decisions formulated to support a particular view, political, economic, etc.,—and for this purpose suppressing altogether or ridiculing and explaining away all other prevailing views. The authors of an indoctrination programme often justify it, with perhaps some foundation, on the ground that the prevailing views are merely the surviving elements of the indoctrination in the past by some interested social or cultural groups. This is really an argument of retaliation. Retaliation prolongs conflict. It is never known to bring about concord. If our educational programme can accustom children to the understanding and use of an analytico-synthetic scheme of classification which is totally exhaustive, it will put in their hands a powerful and impartial tool to detect all the *suppressio veri* and *suggestio falsi* involved in methods of indoctrination. It will reduce credulousness to minimum. It will help to bridge cultural gulf instead of widening it as indoctrination does. The idea is not that formal teaching of an analytico-synthetic classification should be done in schools and colleges. It is enough if the children get accustomed to it. One of the methods of accustoming them is to have the reading materials of libraries arranged and displayed in the stack-room according to an analytico-synthetic classification. The display should be reinforced by an elaborate system of guides—tier guides, gangway guides, bay guides and shelf guides which mention not merely the class numbers which mechanise arrangement but also their meanings in natural language, which alone can produce an impression on the minds of those outside the library profession. Similarly the catalogue too should consist of a classified part in which the entries are arranged according to the same analytico-synthetic classification and plenty of guides are provided mentioning in the proper filiatery order the successive specific subjects, not merely in class numbers but also in words in natural language.

In his paper on *Resolution of cultural conflicts and a master classification* published in the *Abgila* of the Indian Library Association (Volume 2, pages 9 to 18), George Yeisly Rusk of Baltimore goes even further. He envisages the use of a Master classification in organising courses of studies in educationa linstitutions. He thinks that a designation and display of the syllabus according to a good analytico-synthetic classification will enable teachers to know where their courses are truncated and to set them right. Further, co-ordination of the different courses, which a student is obliged to take will be more easy. It will be easier to build up a properly balanced course.

276 Cure

While any educational or cultural work can give only deferred return and has, therefore, to be largely preventive in its nature, a good classification may also be used for immediate resolution of cultural conflicts, though this can be done only to a very limited extent. Display and explanation of classification-charts which bring out the nearness of cultures at deeper invisible levels in spite of their apparent conflict at the superficial level. As Rusk puts it " Whenever any one were even vaguely aware of a cross-relationship between items which at the past had never been worked out, he might study the terminal items and whatever mapped territory lay between them. And whenever one felt like taking an irresponsible jaunt into distant fields, he might do that, returning to his familiar pastures much refreshed for his responsible work for the society, a good analytico-synthetic classification."

277 Conclusion

The fact is that cultural conflict feeds emotional disturbance and perversion of emotions caused by distorted or incomplete knowledge. Cultural concord has to be built on correct understanding through the intellect. Classification is totally bereft of anything emotional and is a dry-as-dust intellectual discipline. The diffusion of classificatory thinking, the presentation of facts and views according to an analytico-synthetic classification and classified display of all reading materials, specimens of arts and crafts and the physical remains of the culture of the past, in museums and exhibitions will generate capacity to understand the cultures of different groups as not antagonistic with one another but as complimentary and harmonising. Thus there is great potentiality in classification to be supplied and used in the intellectual life and development of people so as to promote cultural concord.

CHAPTER 28

Intellectual Team Work

Classification reaches its greatest value in communication in the sphere of intellectual team work. Intellect is an atomising faculty. It analyses and analyses. It narrows extension progressively. It seeks isolating every ultimate constituent part in any pattern. Its contribution to final understanding consists in discovering structural discontinuity *ad infinitum*, arranging the ultimate structural units in a filiatory order, and thus reconstructing the original in such a way that the structural order is not hidden away. In a sense most discoveries and inventions have had to depend upon this atomising and classifying activity of the intellect. A master-mind does these things even without being formally disciplined in it. Flair in reality consists in sensing likeness and unlikeness even of the finest order and classifying in the second sense described in Chapter 12. Those who are poor in flair and those who are not innately creative in their intellectual work can be helped to achieve more than they would otherwise, with the aid of classification in the third sense explained in Chapter 13. A person who is stepped up to a higher level of intellectual work by classificatory aids cannot, of course, achieve much by himself as the range he can cover will be smaller than what is necessary or what is easy for those who can do work in that higher level unaided by classificatory technique. This is not however an irremovable handicap ; for compensation can be had by team work.

281 Vital Existence

Indeed team-work has now become a necessity. Centuries ago many an extension of the field of knowledge was done by stray individuals working in isolation. But in the twentieth century individual discoveries are becoming increasingly rare and difficult to achieve. Perhaps the total background—the total information and knowledge to be carried as apperceptive mass—has now become too vast for most individuals. The number of persons, who have mastery over it, is becoming smaller day by day as a result of the apperceptive load becoming greater day by day. At the same time the work of the world is making an ever-increasing demand on humanity's capacity to discover and to invent. This is because the balance between population pressure and natural resources has been tilted unfavourably to the vital needs of humanity. The raw materials which are directly consumable are proving to be insufficient for the present population. So also is the case with the raw materials that are needed to make consumable commodities. Thus the very vital existence of humanity calls for intellectual team work.

2811 FOOD

The present population of the world cannot find enough food among the fruits, roots and shoots which can be consumed raw. Even the cereals, fish and meat which can be cooked and eaten are not produced in sufficient quantity, if left to nature, without being cultivated. Each farmer ploughing his own field, irrigating it from surface-water or by well-water drawn in the old ways, or finding local manure, alone, is no longer sufficient to produce food in the quantity which humanity needs. Farming has to be on a large scale. Water has to be found in new ways from great depths. The very manure has to be produced artificially on a vast scale. All these need considerable fundamental research in several regions of knowledge. Therefore team work is wanted not only in farming but also to feed the farming work with productive aids.

Moreover the spots on earth where food can be cultivated are unevenly distributed. The distribution of the habitation of men is also uneven. One cannot be made to tally with the other. There is need, therefore, to transport food across the ends of earth. Florida's mangoes have to be transported to the New England States. Danish milk and butter have to feed the British Isles. Australian apples have to reach the Northern Temperate Zone. African coconuts have to be brought to the East Coast of India. Wheat has to be carried half way round the world from places where it is in superfluity to places where there is famine. This world-wide interchange of food materials calls for the solution of many technical problems in transport. The solution of these problems can only be got by team work. The very transport itself has to depend upon team work.

Food has not only to be taken across space but has also to be preserved through time. All seasons are not equally favourable to all kinds of food materials. Nature is rich in food materials in certain seasons. It is fallow in other seasons. When nature gives, its gift has to be accepted and preserved through time.

This problem of storage of food in large quantities and its preservation against bacterial, mycological and entomological attacks requires again considerable fundamental research which can be achieved only by team-work.

Who knows that the day will come when humanity can no longer depend upon the plant and animal kingdom synthesising food materials for it in sufficient quantity. Man may have to synthesise food directly from the elements found in their native condition. Synthetic food may have to be produced. This will again call for research as well as processing on a vast scale, into whose service many persons will have to be pressed. Team work on a scale hitherto unimagined may become necessary.

2812 SHELTER

The present population of the world cannot find enough shelter among the natural caves and groves which can be occupied without any preparation. Even the huts, mud houses and brick houses which can be built and pulled down at will cannot be produced in sufficient quantity as the raw materials needed therefor are not adequate. Technology has to be pressed into service to make building materials by special processes. The manufacture of building materials has to be on a large scale. This needs considerable fundamental research in several regions of knowledge. The large urban concentration of people creates further problems in providing shelter for all. The raw materials needed for processing into building commodities cannot be found on the spot in sufficient quantity. And urban life does not tolerate leisurely raising of buildings. Prefabricated houses have, therefore, come into vogue. Team work is, therefore, wanted to shelter humanity properly.

2813 CLOTHING

The present population of the world cannot find enough skins and bark of trees to clothe themselves. Nor are they prepared to accept such primitive clothing. Clothes woven out of fibres found in nature—plant kingdom or animal kingdom—had come into vogue even in pre-historic times. Today the fibres found in nature have ceased to be sufficient in quantity to clothe all men, and to clothe everything else that man wants to cover with cloth. Artificial fibres have to be made to supplement nature's rescources. Moreover the amount of clothing which a person wears has multiplied several times in recent years. This adds to the quantity of cloth needed. It is no longer possible for each one to spin the yarn and weave the cloth needed, by himself. All this has to be done on a large scale with the help of machinery. Large-scale production brings in its train a number of problems whose solution requires not only technological research but also research in fundamental sciences. This research is not something which a single man can spin out. It needs an army of people working as a team. The machinery used in manufacture also needs a team to tend it.

282 Business Management

The production of materials to meet the increasing vital needs of man have thus necessitated research work in team. This is not, however, the whole story. It is not only technology and the fundamental sciences forming its foundation that call for team work. The large-scale organisation of industry and marketing has itself gone beyond the capacity of a single man whatever be his business acumen. The management of production-plants calls for new techniques. Industrial health, industrial psychology, industrial education, industrial planning and industrial accounts are all new features which call for team work. Commerce or exchange of goods is no longer confined to small areas. The whole world has now become a single unit for commercial purposes. Commerce is no longer on a petty scale. It is on a Himalayan scale. Balance of trade and foreign exchange are two exclusive subjects which the colossal international commerce of today has brought into existence. Both the limbs of business, production and commerce, call for a considerable amount of continuous research. Here again research by a few gifted persons done sporadically at intervals is no longer sufficient. Business research has to be done continuously by large teams of specialists.

283 Social Set-up

Industrialisation began at a time when coal was the chief source of power. This produced a violent disturbance in the distribution of population. Population got massed in certain centres. This produced new social problems both in the crowded cities and in the deserted villages. Rural civic conscience and civic conduct stabilised through centuries have begun to languish because the upper intellectual strata who kept them alive have been mostly withdrawn from villages. Moreover the traditions of rural life depended essentially on intimate living together and community of interest. These were possible in small parishes. These could not be transplanted into urban life where neighbours do not know each other. The social set-up had to be re-organised along more impersonal lines. This has brought several new problems in its train. The attempts to solve these problems have created the new subject of Sociology. During the last 30 years this subject has called for considerable intellectual team work. In villages territorial neighbourliness was the pre-potent bond between persons. It pushed the bond of intellectual or vocational interests into the background. But in urban life the neighbourhood-sense has almost disappeared. Vocational bond is denied the chance to build up intimacy since people working together in a factory or an office are too busy to live intimately with one another during work-hours and get scattered beyond reach of one another after work-hours. Intellectual bond is the only one available. This has to be maintained *in absentia.* There are many other ways in which urbanisation has created sociological problems whose solution calls for intellectual team work.

284 Intellectual Pursuits

It is not only the fundamental sciences, technology, economics and sociology that call for research work in concert by large teams. The purely intellectual discipline of metaphysics too is being put to severe strain by progress in all those subjects. In the past metaphysics thrived lastly on the introspection and the intellectual acumen of gifted individuals.

In them metaphysical pursuit was stimulated by what they could see first hand. When personal experience was the chief feeder to metaphysical speculations these could be individualistic. But today metaphysical pursuit has to reckon with happenings in diverse regions of the ever-expanding field of knowledge. The field of knowledge is expanding both in its extent and intent, both in its area and depth, as a result of world-wide co-ordinated team-work in every other discipline. The result is that metaphysical pursuit itself has had to enter the phase of team-work. Its team-work is even of a more extended kind. It is not merely team-work among philosophers which it needs. It needs also team-work between philosophers on the one side and specialists in diverse subjects on the other. The findings of the latter have all to be gathered, cleaned and dressed, and thrown into their own caldron by the philosophers. The metaphysical distillate which comes out of these has in turn to be tested and assessed by the specialists in different disciplines. The co-operation between philosophers and phsysicists, which has emerged from the physical theories of quanta and fundamental particles, is a remarkable testimony to the co-operative intellectual work which has now come into vogue. The process of cleaning, dressing and distilling has called for great changes in the auxiliary diciplines of logic and epistemology. Indeed the amount of new thought which is being forged by large teams of workers in the field of logic is amazing. General semantics and logical syntax are the result of team-work among Polish and American thinkers on the subject.

285 Quasi-Spiritual Level

Literature and Fine Arts which belong to the quasi-spiritual level have to be always individualistic. In creative work of this kind which draws its sustenance from the spiritual depths of man, team-work is unthinkable. Intuition and organised team-work are perhaps incompatible. No doubt if intuition functions at its best, though each creative person is working by himself, the result will be as if they had worked as a team. But then this does not mean any organised team-work. However, work in such intuitive domains has created an auxiliary domain for intellectual work. Literary criticism, appreciation of music and aesthetics in general belong to this domain. These call for team-work. This is a case of the audience being thrown into a mood for intellectual team-work.

286 Age of Co-operative Research

Thus there is hardly any region in the field of knowledge which can escape the call for intellectual team-work. It can indeed be said that the world has now entered the age of co-operative research. This is more visible in developed countries like U. K., U. S. A. and U. S. S. R. It has not yet become visible in undeveloped countries like India and other Asian countries. In India we speak of lack of man-power. By this we do not mean paucity of human beings. We mean only scarcity of men capable of throwing themselves into a co-operative research team. On the other hand when the developed countries speak of lack of man-power, they mean that co-operative research has assumed dimensions which require more men than the country has. For example, it was recently reported that team-work in scientific research had absorbed the scientifically trained men of the U. K. so fully that teachers of science could not be found by the schools and that teaching of science got dangerously curtailed.

2861 BEGINNINGS OF TEAM-WORK

The economy of team-work on a large scale was first put into practice by industrial magnates like Ford. The marvellous achievement of team-work was witnessed by me when I was in one of the automobile manufacturing companies of U. S. A. The factory is so carefully laid out. The rails and the moving ropes are all perfectly registered. The workmen are spaced out at right intervals. The job to be done by each is accurately pre-determined. Starting at one end where raw materials are assembled right through to the other end where the test-driver darts out in the finished car, it takes but a few hours. This is team-work which I could never have imagined by merely reading about it in books. The co-efficient of efficiency which it yields and the profit it brings are indeed marvellous. Here what is visible is team-work in the physical plane.

2862 EXTENSION TO INTERLOCKED UNITS

This experience within a single unit of production naturally led to the spread-out of team-work among several interlocked units. The General Electric Company, The Westing House and the Standard Oil Company have spread out the magic mat of team-work over several plants located at great distances. Utilisation of waste-products has been acting as an urge to link up several industrial concerns by the spirit of team-work.

2863 INTERLOCKING OF RESEARCH AND PRODUCTION

Prompted by the benefits which accrue from team-work at the physical level, the big industrial bodies have begun to throw into their team squads of intellectual workers engaged in applied as well as fundamental research. This is a development of less than half a century. Hundreds of individual industrial concerns in the developed countries have now a research sub-team as part of their general team. This kind of interlocking of work at research and production levels is proving to be necessary as well as profitable. I was amazed at the reciprocal benefit which pure research and business interests derive by such inter-locking. Let me give an example. During war, quartz crystals occurring in nature were nearing exhaustion. The business of the Bell Telephone Company depended essentially on the use of quartz crystals. Its production wing had therefore to look to its research-wing to come to its rescue. Work went on for a few years. When I visited them, artificial growth of quartz crystals had become an accomplished fact. I could see, in the gleaming eyes of the members of this section of the research-wing, the satisfaction described by Valmiki in his *Ramayana* as evident in the gleaming eyes of Viswamitra when Sita's marriage with Rama was accomplished. In the same company as well as in the University of California at Los Angeles I saw how such a distant piece of work as that of designing of complicated calculating machines had been woven into a large piece of team-work leading to an enrichment of every element in the team.

2864 EXTRA-MURAL TEAM-WORK

Political and profit motives do put barriers beyond which certain types of information should not be allowed to go. In spite of this, several business bodies are able to find sectors in which they can co-operate with profit. They find that there is economy in such co-operation. This economy brings them mutual benefit. The Atira (Ahmedabad Textile Industries Research Association) is an example of such extra-mural team-work among textile business houses. There are many such central research institutes maintained by several industries in the developed countries. Here the production is all done by each business house in its own way and even in competition with the others. But some of the intellectual work in the fundamental fields is provided for jointly by all of them. This enlargement of the sector of team-work is coming more and more into vogue.

2865 INTERNATIONAL TEAM-WORK

Except during international tension or war, co-operative research covers several countries. During the last decade the needs of war put the seal of secrecy on most intellectual work and prevented it from getting interlocked across national boundaries. The intellectual workers had to submit themselves to it though under protest. The moment war ended all the scientific organisations rebelled against the continuation of any national exclusiveness in intellectual pursuit. The scientists said that there was no national boundary in scientific work. They insisted on intellectual team-work being spread over the whole earth.

287 Age of Communication

Intellectual team-work covering such a large range of subjects and interests and spread over vast geographical areas has to depend essentially on accurate and rapid communication between the workers in the several groups in the team. Every micro-unit of thought created in any spot within the team should be broadcast to every other spot in the team. Apart from occasional urgent communication being done through wire or wireless, routine communication among a group of intellectual workers is effected through print. International communication and communication within a country of nascent thought are effected through periodicals. The number of periodicals which was about 10,000 about a century ago has now mounted up to about 100,000. This is a measure of the dependence of intellectual team-work on communication. Our age may well be called the Age of Communication.

2871 INTERNATIONAL COMMUNICATION

Apart from international and national extramural communication, many of the industrial houses have their own house-periodicals to effect communication among their own workers. These are of two kinds. First there are those which circulate local abstracts of the important articles occurring in the periodicals taken by the house, which have a bearing on the work in progress in the house. The second variety circulates confidentially within the house the nascent thought produced by the staff of the house. It is difficult to estimate the number of such house-periodicals current in the world today.

2872 PROJECT REPORTS

Another important material for communication which is being continuously built up and kept on file in most industrial houses consists of the reports of the research projects set up in the house. These reports are not only of contemporary value, *i.e.*, when its contents are in a nascent state, but also of deferred value. Some of the houses have several running feet of volumes of such reports of research projects. They are mostly unique typewritten copies. Their presence saves industrial houses a good deal of money which should have been wasted in repetitive work but for their being communicated across time.

2873 TRANSLATED CONTENTS PERIODICAL

Before the First World War most of the nascent micro-units of thought were expressed in two or three European languages. After that war several other European languages and particularly those of the Slavonic family have come to be used as media. As the people who could read the foreign languages which have newly come into vogue is small and as the number of periodicals in any specific subject far exceeds the financial capacity of most of the libraries, there is a natural tendency to procure only particular articles which are of interest and get them translated.

To facilitate selection, a new practice is being adopted. It is to publish periodically translations of the contents-pages of periodicals in foreign languages. An example is *Translated contents lists of Russian periodicals and list of translations available at the Science Museum Library* published by the Department of Scientific and

Industrial Research of Great Britain. The issue for October 1950 of this periodical, for example, gives the contents of recent issues of each of 28 Russian periodicals in diverse subjects translated into English language. At the end of the contents of each periodical, the name of the personal or the corporate author responsible for the translation is given as a note. For example the Scot Polar Research Institute of Cambridge is stated to be responsible for the contents-page of the Russian *Bulletin* of the All-Union Geographical Society. A further co-ordination which leads to economy in carrying communication in intellectual team-work across linguistic boundaries is illustrated by the Union Card Index of Technical Translations being developed by the Science-Technology Group of Special Libraries Association in U. S. A. The index gives information on any technical translations from any language into English in the field of applied sciences. It is arranged alphabetically by the author and includes translations found in private industry as well as learned or public bodies and professional translation agencies.

2874 COMMUNICATION OF INDIVIDUAL ARTICLES

The peculiar type of periodicals mentioned in Section 2873 enables workers to spot out the articles which are likely to fall within their field of interest. Technical processes have now been developed to procure copies of individual articles which are required. These processes are being improved and made cheaper day by day. Photostat copies, microfilm, microfilm-strips, micro cards, etc., are the forms of mechanical reproduction which have already become familiar. Thus communication is being rendered so effective that even particular pages can be communicated to workers on request. National Documentation Centres are trying to remove all kinds of difficulties in carrying communication to this nice degree of intimacy and personal requirement. Legal difficulties pertaining to copyright are being explored and removed. Considerable research is also going on to improve the technical processes.

2875 TELETYPING

Another development, which may be expected to become common very soon in making communication effective and expeditious between members doing intellectual team-work though scattered within a country or even on the entire surface of the earth, is teletyping. The daily press is already using this method extensively in communicating news and often even long speeches and documents. Considerable international co-ordination has been already thus effected in regard to political and common news. Of course it is the volume of information transmitted in this way which makes it economical. The volume is great because what is transmitted is intended for the consumption of the common man. But information to be communicated within a team of intellectual workers will hardly ever attain an economic volume to be handled in the way in which press news are handled. However, scientific departments like those of meteorology and the business transport, particularly air transport, are adopting this means of communication. Assuming that communication between intellectual workers can be expedited by teletyping, the main problem to be considered will be the correct enunciation of what is required and the search for it among the materials stacked in libraries. We shall consider this problem in the next section.

288 Classification and Planned Search

A few days ago I was sitting in the sun in the open lawn in front of my house and working on this book. Suddenly sunlight was cut out. An extensive shadow fell on the ground. It was obvious that it could not have been caused by distant clouds. The feeling came that it was due to smoke. If there could be such thick smoke most of Delhi should have been on fire. A shiver of fear went through me and I looked up. It was not smoke. It was not clouds. It was a swarm of locusts flying within a hundred feet of height. These tiny living insects began to spread over Delhi so thickly and so extensively that they could cut out sunlight. So it is with the swarm of articles embodying nascent thought being created to-day and spread over intellectual team-work.

2881 BEGINNINGS OF COMMUNICATION

Before the invention of printing the spoken word was the supreme means of communication of scientific knowledge. Manuscript books embodying only micro-units of thought supplemented it. This supplement was necessary because some needed to go back to the same communication again and again to get the full benefit of it or even to understand it. The spoken word being evanescent, the help of the manuscript had to be sought. Manuscript being a laborious affair, there were not many manuscripts available to stifle communication by their very number.

In spite of it, Tennyson pictures Lucretius feeling smothered when going

"To turn and ponder those three hundred scrolls
Left by the Teacher, whom he held divine"

The invention of printing gradually swelled the number of embodiments of macro-units of thought. Even within a century after the invention of printing, the number of whole books had become so vast that the need was felt for a special tool for search. Konrad Gesner of Zurich supplied this tool by compiling his *Bibliotheca universalis*, a folio of 1,300 pages listing about 12,000 books known to him. He published this in 1545. But within three years he found that it proved to be too futile a tool for search. He sensed that it would not serve its purpose unless the aid of classification was taken. He therefore brought out in 1548 a classified version of his bibliography under the title *Pandectarum sive partititonum universalium*. This act of Gesner has great significance today.

2882 EMERGENCE OE PERIODICALS

The *Transactions* of the Royal Society of London which began in 1765 marks the beginning of a new means of communication among those engaged in intellectual team-work. It was the periodical. From the eighteenth century onwards. Country after country began to adopt this means of communication. The Academy of Sciences of St. Petersburgh (now Leningrad) sent out the first issue of its *Memoires* in 1725. The Royal Swedish Academy and the Royal Danish Academy projected their respective *Proceedings* in 1739 and 1745. The *Verhandlungan* of the Royal Academy of Science at Gottingen started off as the first German periodical in 1752. Benjamin Franklin established the *Transactions* of the American Philosophical Society in 1771. Even provincial towns started their periodicals about the end of the eighteenth century. For example the Manchester Literary and Philosophical Society founded its *Memoires* in 1789. Till the beginning of the nineteenth century the periodicals were encyclopaedic in scope. They contained fairly long monographs. Their number too was small.

2883 EMERGENCE OF SPECIALISED PERIODICALS

The nineteenth century saw the emergence of periodicals specialising in specific subjects instead of covering the whole field of knowledge. The mathematical periodical was brought into vogue by *Crelles journal* in 1826. The flood of specialised chemical periodicals which is swamping us today was heralded by Leibig's *Annalen der Pharmazie* which was started in 1832. In Physics alone 80 periodicals were floated between 1810 and 1910.

2884 PRESENT POSITION

Specialisation among periodicals has become much more pronounced today. In the nineteenth century periodials covered at least the whole of what we are now accustomed to call a main class of knowledge. But today we have periodicals on even such narrow sub-divisions of main classes as Flavouring Icecream. Apart from this the swarm of articles has swollen like a swarm of locusts. It is estimated that about 2,000,000 articles are now produced every year by intellectual team-work. These are embodied in about 100,000 periodicals. This flood of micro-units of thought has brought a problem of its own in it train. We can understand the problem if we remember that no intellectual worker can give of his best in isolation. He has to live chiefly on the printed word. It is by communication through periodicals that an intel lectual worker has to be helped and inspired by a fellow-worker in his team whom he may never have seen and who lives thousands of miles away. Indeed it is the periodical literature that binds workers in the same specific subject into a team. But the spate of articles is now such that it is becoming extremely difficult to get abreast of the communication which pours forth even in the most limited sector of the narrowest specific subject. The spate is such that research libraries almost double in number every ten years. It is not absence of nascent thought which we now suffer from. It is their plethora. Our method of search among them is an outmoded one. It is this which causes trouble today. Quick and effective application of the knowledge, both as a step from which further advances can be made and for efficient industrial and social development, depends largely upon its being properly assembled and on the provision of efficient tools for search.

2885 ASSEMBLING FOR SEARCH

When several articles are to be stored and to be drawn from time to time according to needs, it is but common sense that we should assemble them in a way that will facilitate search. What will facilitate search naturally depends upon the purpose for which the articles will be used and the particular combination in which they are likely to be used. If we take the articles in a household, for example, we put all food materials together in and near the kitchen, the clothes together in the wardrobe and the reading materials together in the study room. In the wardrobe again we subdivide the clothes into groups and assemble them in a helpful way. We put all the summer-wear together and the winter-wear separately together. This division and subdivision will have to be continued to the necessary degree. Probably the winter-wear will be sorted out either into coats, pants, shirts and so on if they are all of the same colour and pattern, or all the pieces of a suit may be clubbed together and the several suits may be arranged in some helpful order according to their make or pattern. This is classification in the second sense as described in Chapter 12. This much wiil be sufficient in dealing with physical articles, because their likeness and unlikeness, which determine the position of each article in the assemblage will be obvious to the primary senses. It is not so in the assemblage of the printed embodiments of micro-units of thought or even the assemblage of the catalogue entries describing them. What can be apprehended by the primary senses misses the soul or thet hought-content which is the thing sought. It is, therefore, necessary to invoke the aid of ordinal numbers—classificatory language—to asssemble the articles. Moreover the number of units to be assembled is ever-growing—potentially infinite. This neessitates that the scheme of classification should have infinite hospitality in array and chain and should be analytico-synthetic and expressive.

2886 WHAT TO SEARCH

Apart from assembling articles so as to make search easy, we also want help in ascertaining what articles a consumer wishes to have. Here again in the case of physical articles their very presence and their being readily distinguishable by primary senses, form sufficient help. But in the case of articles embodying micro-units of thought the consumer is denied this kind of physical help. He needs help in the exact and expeditious enunciation of his requirements. Few readers are able to name their specific subjects exactly. It is a broader or a narrower subject that is usually thought of. It is the duty of the library to start with whatever he brings up, however wide of the mark it may be, and guide him to the exact specific subject and reading materials which will satisfy his vaguely expressed wants. Classification—particularly an analytico-synthetic expressive classification—is one of the well-tried aids in this matter. The expressiveness of the class number, the standing-in-relief of its facets and phases, and the sharpness of the foci in the different facets will form an excellent probe in the hands of the library to determine the exact requirements of the consumer.

2887 SECONDARY AIDS FOR SEARCH

Viewed this way, classification is an aid for search. But it has some limitations. Classification facilitates search merely by arranging the articles in helpful order with the aid of class numbers. But as class numbers have to be ordinal numbers, they are cyphers which convey no meaning to the reader and fail by themselves to give the necessary aid for search. These difficulties are mitigated (1) in the stack-room, by putting up guides of various sorts—tier guides, gangway guides, bay guides and shelf guides—all bilingual guides mentioning the names of subjects in both classificatory and natural languages ; and (2) in the classified part of the catalogue, by inserting bilingual guide-cards in a similar manner. The names in the natural language are intelligible to the reader. The names in the classificatory language only act, if at all, as remembrancers that there is an order aimed at in the arrangement ; and they may be even ignored by the reader. To know where to land on the classified part of the catalogue or where to begin in the stack-room without undue fumbling about in starting his search, the reader should be helped by translating the word he uses to express his subject—be it specific or more extensive or less extensive than what he really needs—into the class number. The alphabetical part of the ctalogue is needed to do this.

288 Conclusion

Thus we find that in alliance with a good alphabetical key which gives the meanings of terms belonging to natural language translated into the artificial classificatory language, classification can be made an adequate tool in searching the embodiments of micro-units of thought which any intellectual worker may require at any time. By thus providing for planned search— planning beginning even at the stage of assemblage and the same plan being of use at all stages of service—classification can be of immense help to communication and is necessary in intellectual team-work. Last summer I was brought into contact with a new industrial organisation which had not yet gone beyond the stage of industrial research. This being the first body to exploit a new element for industrial purposes, the entire team of workers was concentrated practically under one roof. The help which this team could get from anybody else in the world was negligibly small. But already the difficulties of communication within this closed team of intellectual workers had assumed great dimensions. The person in charge of the files of the findings of the members of this industrial laboratory felt beyond depth. The research-workers themselves felt similarly and leaned more and more on the person in charge of the files. Having tried the D. C., the U. D. C. and the Congressional Classification and failing to find much help from them, that person turned to the Colon Classification. My presence in the United States synchronised with this phase of the development of communication in that industrial research organisation. I was therefore taken into consultation. It is the experience which this brought to me which convinced me beyond doubt of the great part that a good expressive analytico-synthetic classification is going to play in the maintenance of effective, expeditious communication among those engaged in intellectual team-work.

Part 3

Classification and its Future

CHAPTER 31

Domains in Communication

Communication itself falls in the domain of social relation. Social relation requires a minimum of two human beings. At the other extremity it can cover the entire human species. In social relation, communication concerns transfer or exchange of mental activities. Mental activities which are to be communicated may belong solely to the category of emotions or solely to the category of thought or to a mixture of these two.

311 Emotion

Emotion is at its best in its nascent state. It is therefore best communicated immediately by behaviour. This behaviour may include utterances of explosive sounds. Even words may get imbedded in such an explosive utterance. But often the thought-content of the word does not count. For example, when an angry man calls his opponent " Ass," " Bastard " or " Goose " they are not vehicles of thought but only of emotion. Similarly when a fondling mother calls her child " Honey," " Kid" or "Treasure" they are not vehicles of thought but only of emotion. When the mystic Sundarar warbled out the words, " Mad man," " Sugar-cane " and " Treacherous man " in addressing God, they were not vehicles of thought but only of emotion.

312 Thought

Thought, on the other hand, can be stored and communicated long after its production. Indeed we speak of cold thought. In the case of a mixture of thought and emotion, communication gains in efficiency by proximity and by the use of all forms of behaviour and all the primary senses at once. But when pure thought alone is involved, the help of these factors is not necessary. It is communication of pure thought with which we are concerned in this book. Pure thought, it may be emphasised, may even be 'thought on emotion.' For example, when a person writes to a friend who is not within his reach saying "I am angry with you," it is not emotion 'anger' which is communicated. It is only 'the thought of his being angry' that is communicated. We have, therefore, to distinguish between emotion *qua* emotion and 'thought of emotion.' In part 2 we examined the spheres in which pure emotion, mixture of emotion and thought, and pure thought are usually communicated. We singled out intellectual team-work as the sphere in which pure thought is communicated. We also showed that in the sphere of cultural concord 'thought about emotion' may have to loom large. In the sphere of commercial contact we saw that it is pure thought, in the immediate presence of concrete objects forming the subject matter of thought, which is involved.

313 Thought-Transfer

To arrive at the domain of classification in communication, it will be helpful if the proess of communication is examined, the various domains in the process are isolated, and the dominant factors in each of those domains are stated. In isolating the domains in the process of communication, we shall take the help of diagrams. In the diagrams a vertical line represents the state in which thought lies or the embodiment which it has taken. Each vertical line is for convenience denoted by a capital letter A, B, C . . . X, Y, Z. A single arrow between two consecutive vertical lines stands for 'Transformation.' The domain of a transformation is indicated by a letter-pair. For example, BC stands for the domain in which transformation takes place from the state or embodiment B to the state or embodiment C of thought. A couple of arrows is used to denote transfer of thought *qua* thought or of an embodiment of thought across space or time. The region of transfer is indicated by a letter-pair representing the two ends of transfer. The person who originates thought will be denoted by the term 'Producer.' The person who receives thought for use will be denoted by the term 'Consumer.' The person who transforms thought from one state or embodiment to another will be denoted by the term 'Transformer.' The person who transfers thought or an embodiment of thought across space or time will be denoted by the term 'Carrier.' Terms like transforming apparatus, transformation-aid, transfer-apparatus and transfer-aid will be self-explanatory in the context in which they occur.

314 Direct Thought-Transfer

In the present stage of human evolution unmediated thought-transfer may be assumed to be not commonly practicable. In section 265 reference was made to the limiting form in which there can be direct thought-transfer unmediated by any aid whatever. H. G. Wells has pictured it in his *Men like gods*. Incidence of direct thought-transfer is a subject of study in metapsychology. In such cases the diagramatic representation will take the following form :

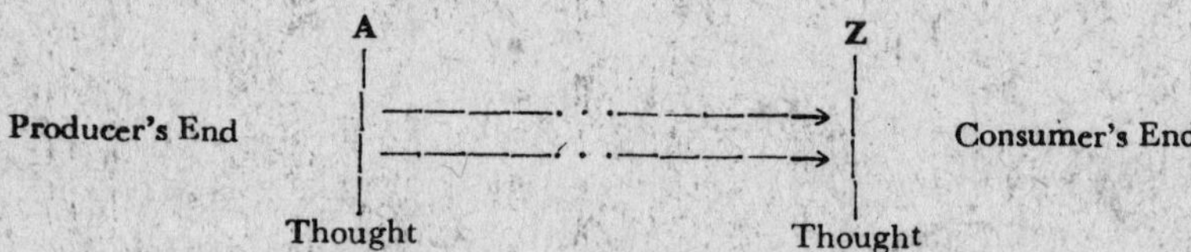

We have only the producer and the consumer figuring in the communication. Nothing is known about the transfer-apparatus. Classification owns no known or explicit domain in direct thought-transfer.

315 Transformation into Language

In practice thought has to be transferred through a series of media, and not directly. The media call for successive transformations and re-transformations. In all known cases, thought has first to be expressed in a language : in other words, it has to be embodied in language ; we may say that thought is transformed into language. The transformer in this domain is normally the producer himself. Occasionally thought may, in the first instance, be transformed by the producer into gestures, and somebody else may embody it in language. But this is a rare exception. In any case, transformation of thought into language is effected at the producer's end. The language has then to be transferred. At the consumer's end, the language has to be re-transformed into thought.

3151 DIRECT LANGUAGE-TRANSFER

In such cases the diagramatic representation will take the following form :

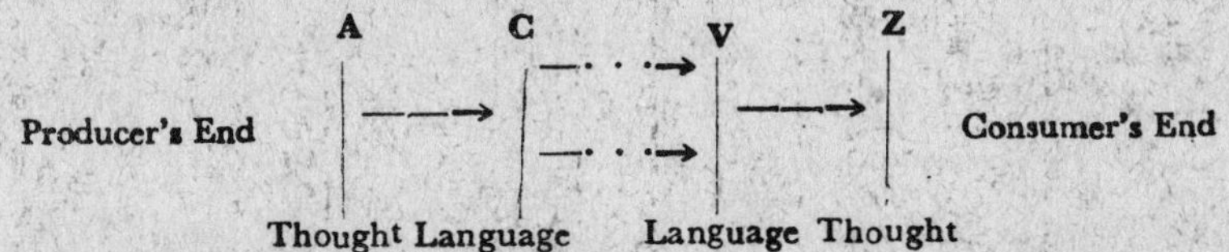

Normally the transformer in the domain AC is the producer himself and that in the domain VX is the consumer himself. The transformation-aid is either simple imitation or the more complex process of learning the use of a language. In the domain CV unmediated language-transfer is not possible. Classification owns no known or explicit domain in direct language-transfer.

316 Transformation of Language

Language has to be first transformed at the producer's end into something else and re-transformed into itself—after transfer—at the consumer's end. Various transformations are possible for this purpose. Three of them will be considered, to begin with.

3161 TRANSFORMATION INTO SOUND WAVES

Language may be transformed at the producer's end into sound waves. These may be transferred to the consumer through the medium of matter such as air and may be re-transformed by him into language and thought successively. In such cases the diagramatic representation will take the following form:

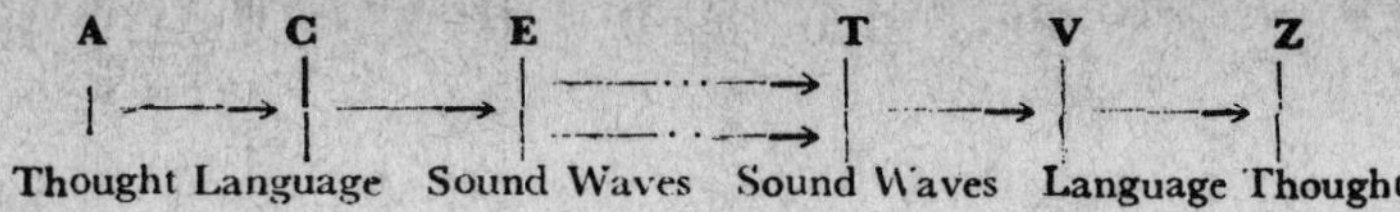

The transformation takes place in the domain CE. The transformer is often the producer himself. The means are imitation and learning. The re-transformation in the domain TV is similar. The re-transformation has to be made at the very moment when the sound-wave reaches the consumer. For embodiment in sound-wave is evanescent and cannot be preserved *qua* sound-wave. Further one and only one such embodiment normally reaches the consumer at any one moment. If more than one reach him, the others usually amount to noise. Noise is avoided when communication is effected by this means. As there is only a single thought-mass which is within the reach of the consumer at any one time, classification can find no domain in thought-language-transfer through the medium of sound-waves alone. For classification pre-supposes the existence of at least two entities.

3162 TRANSFORMATION INTO RECORD

A second process is for the language to be transformed at the producer's end into a written or printe d state,—*i.e.* into a material called 'record.' This may be transferred to the consumer and may be re-transformed by him into language and thought successively. The material in which record is normally made in modern times is paper. Recording is in terms of letters written or printed. It is printed record that we have to deal with frequently. In such cases the diagramatic representation will take the following form :

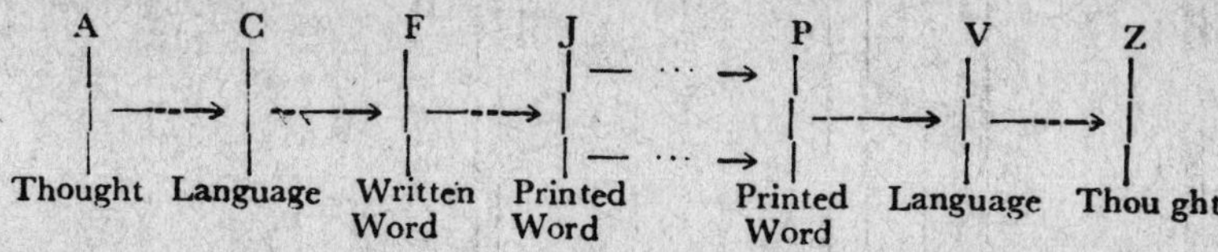

The transformation takes place in the domains CF and FJ. In the domain CF the transformer is the producer either by himself or in company with a secretary. The necessary means is literacy. In the domain FJ the transformer is the printer. The means is the art of printing. In the domain JP the record is carried physically from J to P. In the domain PV literacy is the means and the transformer is ordinarily the consumer himself.

3163 TRANSFORMATION INTO SOUND RECORD

A third process is for the language to be transformed at the producer's end first into sound-waves and these into sound-records. The plates containing the sound-records may be transferred to the consumer by physical transport and may be re-transformed by him into language and thought successively. In such cases the diagramatic representation will take the following form :

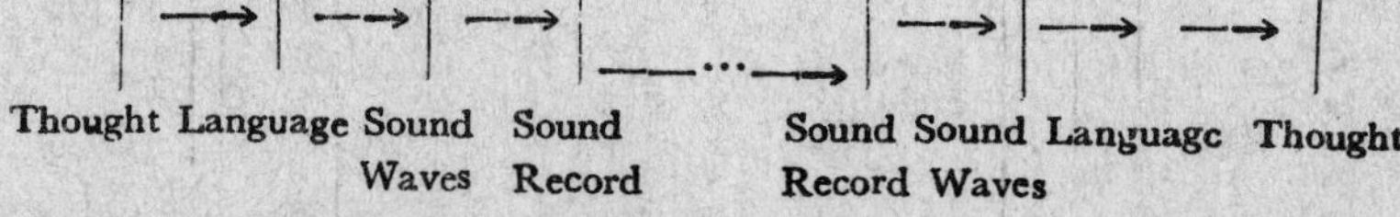

The above diagram is like the diagram in section 3161

for transformation into sound-waves with the insertion of an additional transformation into the sound-records at G and an additional re-transformation of the sound-record at R into sound-waves. The additional transformation takes place in the domain EG. Here the transformer is the sound-engineer and the means of transformation is the machinery for recording. The additional re-transformation takes place in the domain RT. In this the transformer can be the consumer himself. The means of transformation is the gramophone machine.

317 Additional Transformation

To secure greater efficiency or for other reasons, it may be possible to introduce additional domains of transformation at the producer's end and of re-transformation at the consumer's end.

3171 USE OF RADIO

For example, in relation to section 3161 the sound waves may be transformed into radio-waves. These may be transferred to the consumer's end across space. These may then be re-transfomed into sound-waves. In such cases the diagramatic representation will take the following form:

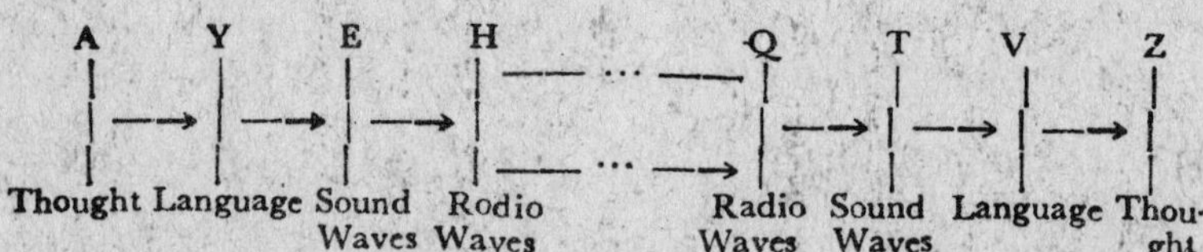

In the domain EH the transformer will be the radio-engineer. The means of transformation will be radio-technology. Similar remarks apply to the domain QT where radio-waves are re-transformed into sound-waves.

3172 USE OF MICRO-FILM

In relation to section 3162 the printed record may be transformed into micro-films. These may be transferred physically to the consumer's end. They may then be re-transformed into language. In such cases the diagramatic representation will take the following form :

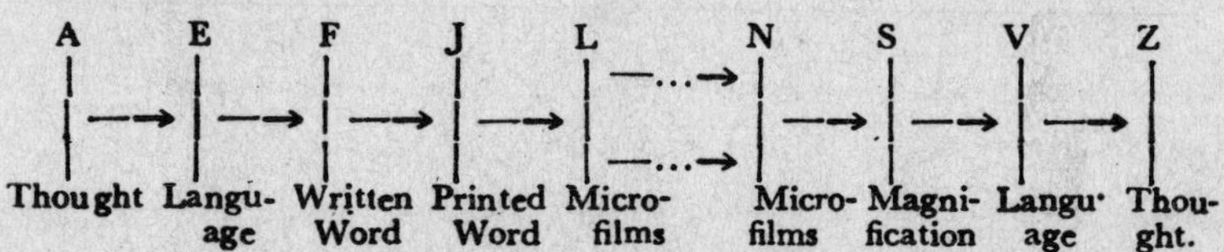

In the domain JL the transformer will be the film-producer. The means of transformation will be film-technology. In the domain NS the transformer is the technician. In the domain SV the transformer will be the consumer himself. The means of transformation will be the machinery called 'reader' and literacy.

3173 USE OF TRANSLATION

In all cases where the language of the consumer is different from that of the producer, it will be necessary to make a further transformaion—translation from the producer's language to the consumer's language. This is best done at the consumer's end. In the diagrams of all the sections exeept that of 314, the diagramatic representation of the extreme part of the consumer's end will take the following form :

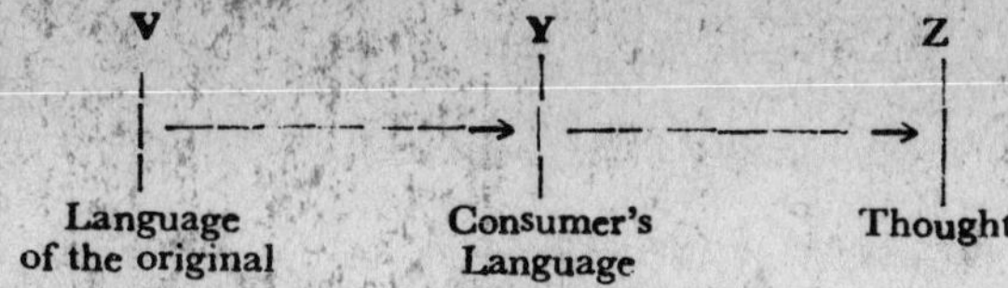

In the domain VY the transformer will be the translator. The means of transformation will be translation. This will require knowledge of both the languages and at least some understanding of the thought. In the domain YZ the transformer will be the consumer.

3174 USE OF CIPHER

In diplomatic communications, the thought may be transformed from language to cipher and the cipher may be transferred to the consumer's end. Here the cipher may be re-transformed into language and thought successively. We shall also presume that the cipher will be transferred by teletyping. In such cases the diagramatic representation may take the following form:

In the domain CD the transformer will be the cipher-specialist and the transformation is called 'coding.' In the domain DH the transformer will be the teletypist working in collaboration with the radio-engineer. The means of trasformation will be radio-technology. In the domain HQ the transfer will be in the form of radio waves. In the domain QU the transformer will be the radio-engineer and the means of transformation will be radio-technology. In the domain UV the cipher-specialist will be the transformer and the transformation is called "de-coding."

318 Comparison of Domains

Since classification is essentially concerned with subject matter or thought *qua* thought, as a preliminary to fix the domain of classification, it may be helpful to examine how thought figures in the different domains in communication. Perhaps it is useful to recall in this connection that a printed material may be taken to have a soul (=thought), a subtle body (=language spoken or written) and a gross body (=physical matter in which the language is written or printed). It can be seen that a full knowledge of the thought-content is necessary in the domain AC and that capacity to consume the thought-content is necessary in the domain VZ, as marked in all the diagrams of this chapter except the first. In the domain AC it is the producer that should have this knowledge while in the domain VZ it is the consumer that should have the capacity to consume the thought-content. In the domains CE and CF at the producer's end and the domains PV and SV at the consumer's end, a complete knowledge of language is necessary on the part of the transformers. Some knowledge of thought will be helpful. In the domains FJ, EG, EH, FL, JL and DH at the producer's end and in the domains ST, RT, NU and QU at the consumer's end, there is no need at all to have any knowledge of thought-content. So also it is in the domains of transfer JP, GS, HR, LN and HQ. Thus, if at all, classification can find foothold only in the domains AE and AF at the producer's end and PZ, SZ, NZ and SZ at the consumer's end. We shall call these 'Potential Zones for Classification's Domain'. We shall see in the next Chapter in what way classification can actually establish a domain of its own in its potential zones in communication.

CHAPTER 32

Domain of Classification

We shall first confine ourself to the potential zone at the consumer's end. So long as communication presents thought to the consumer in an evanescent embodiment like sound-waves there is only one thought-form in the consumer's zone at any one time. As it has been already stated in section 3161, no aid is necessary to pick it up. Communication is completed without the formation of any other domain at consumer's end. All that is needed is that the consumer should have the capacity to recognise the thought *qua* thought.

321 Apupa Pattern

If, on the other hand, communication presents thought at the consumer's end in a storeable material embodiment like records, many thought-forms get crowded in the potential zone of that end. Jamming sets in very soon. Picking out what is wanted is no easy task. Communication does not get completed unless facilities are provided for organising the records and keeping them arranged in a helpful order, so that what may be wanted at any movement can be picked out expeditiously, exhaustively, and exactly, that is without any unwanted record also coming along and hampering consumption. If any unwanted record does come along, it will cause distraction. It will be equivalent to noise. We shall for convenience refer to it as 'irrelevant record.' The boundary-line between irrelevant and relevant records is not sharp and clear-cut. Various degrees of intensity are possible in the relevance and irrelevance of records. A totally or intimately relevant record may be called "Umbral Record." A partially irrelevant record may be called "Penumbral Record." A totally irrelevant record may be called "Alien Record." The Umbral, Penumbral and Alien records arrive at random at the consumer's end and will lie at the point P, R, N, or U as the case may be. To make them readily seizable, they should be arranged in a helpful order,—*i.e.*, in the order Alien, Penumbral, Umbral, Penumbral and Alien—so that all the most relevant records are in the centre and the other records stand fanned out oneither side of the centre in decreasing order of their relevance. We shall call such an arrangement an "Apupa Arrangement." Apupa arrangement has to be linear.

322 Everywhere-Apupa

The arrangement should be "Everywhere-Apupa"—*i.e.*, whatever region or point in the line is taken as umbral by the consumer, he should find all the records fanned out in apupa pattern. In other words it should be apupa to every consumer whatever be the umbral region of his interest. A strictly everywhere-apupa pattern is the ideal. In actuality, we should make as close an approximation as possible to this ideal. The formation of such a pattern has to be part of the process of communication. It is the formation of such a pattern which has been called classification in the third sense in chapter 13.

3212 FIRST DOMAIN OF CLASSIFICATION

Classification is equivalent to an embodiment of

the thought-content of each record, lying at P, R, N, or U as the case may be, in a classificatory language, *i.e.*, language of class numbers, *i.e.*, an artificial language of ordinal numbers. When the thought-content is so embodied, the class number can be put on the record concerned. Then the records are transformed into classed records and can be arranged mechanically by their class numbers. Classification is thus a transformation of thought. This change in arrangement from accession or random order to apupa order is itself a subsidiary transformation. This is the first use of classification in the process of communication. Here is a diagramatic representation of what happens at the consumer's end when we are handling printed records.

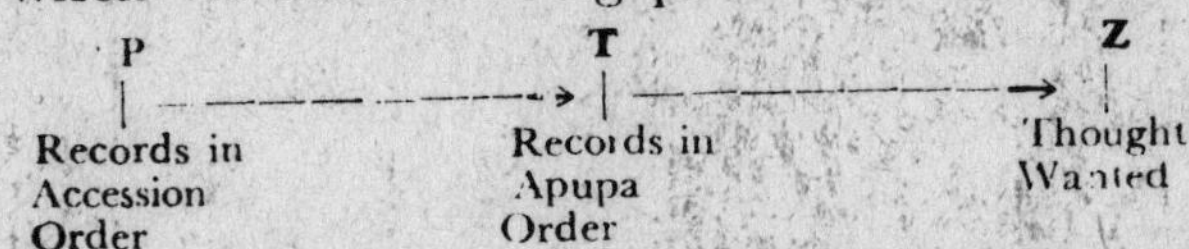

PT is a domain of classification. The transformer is the classifier. The means is the Classification Scheme. At T the records lie, as near as possible, in the everywhere-apupa pattern, whereas they are in random order at P. In the way in which they lie at P, communication is difficult since it is difficult to pick out the records that should be re-transformed into thought at Z. But in the way in which they lie at T, picking out the needed materials is easy. There is no jamming. Communication is facilitated.

3214 NEED FOR GUIDES

Records do not readily lay bare their thought-contents. These cannot be read out at a glance. The call numbers written on them constitute a cipher-language. This is not easily intelligile to the consumer. It is therefore necessary to put up guides to help the consumer. All records which are embodiments of the same thought-mass will share one guide between themselves. This guide should name the equivalent of the class number in natural language. It is also desirable that the guide should mention the class number. This will help the consumer to follow the apupa pattern from end to end with greater comfort and incidentally accustom him to the use of class numbers.

3215 NEED FOR CATALOGUE

A consumer who comes looking for records embodying a specific thought-mass should be readily led to his umbral region. If he is not so helped, he may have to waste time and energy in finding it. When we go to a large dinner party, we appreciate the seats being numbered, a diagram of the seating arrangement being put up at the entrance and near it a guide showing our names in alphabetical order with our seat-numbers entered against them. In the case of consumers of thought, it is not merely a comfort; it is almost a necessity. It is the business of the catalogue to provide this help. It is the Class Index Entries in the catalogue which provide this help. The leading sections in such entries are in natural language. Class Index Entries therefore lie in the alphabetical part of the catalogue. Each class index entry says, as it were, "For the records on the specific thought-mass named in my leading section, start at that point of the apupa pattern at T, where the following class number occurs."

322 Second Domain for Classification

As physical records of thought-masses take space, the shelf-length occupied by them often becomes too vast for a convenient sweep by the eye. If, to reduce the space to be scanned, the record is reduced to micro-cards or films, the writing on them is too small to be picked up by the eye. Magnifying them and scanning them by one sweep of the eye is even more difficult. It therefore becomes necessary to represent the records by entries in a catalogue, even as it is to represent the seats by marks in a plan. To be helpful, a part of the catalogue should present the entries in the same apupa order as the one in which the records themselves are arranged at T. The entries in this part of the catalogue have, therefore, class numbers in their leading sections. It is called the Classified Part of the Catalogue.

3221 SUBJECT ANALYTICALS

It often happens that some of the records embody more than one thought-mass. They are multi-focal and not uni-focal, in the terminology developed in section 147. The record being an ultimate physical unit, it can not be torn into parts corresponding to each of the foci, in order to give each part its appropriate place in the apupa pattern at T. When we are in this predicament, the classified part comes to our aid. It agrees to put up a separate entry for each of the different foci embodied within one record—a Cross-Reference Entry. A cross-reference entry contains the class number of a component focus in the leading section and says, as it were, " For the specific subject represented by the class number in the leading section, *see also* pages so and so of such and such record marked with such and such call number and lying in the region of the apupa arrangement, which is marked by the class-number part of it."

3222 LOOPLINE IN COMMUNICATION

The catalogue thus functions as a loop-line in the progress of communication. It occurs alongside the domain PT of the main line. This loop-line in communication forms the second domain of classification. It is obvious that this loop-line becoming a second domain of classification is contingent on the main line of communication having allowed a domain for classification.

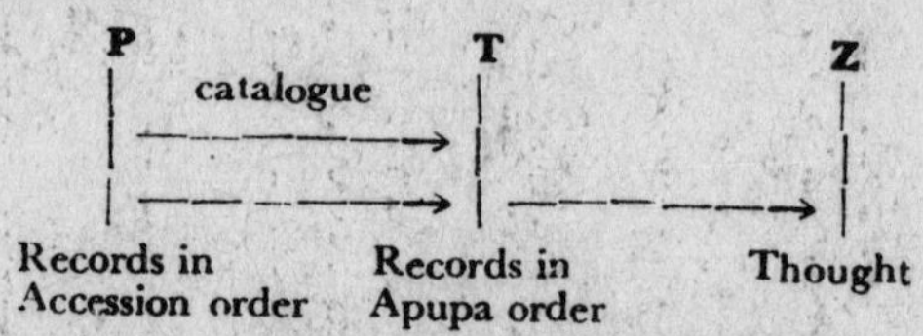

32221 Historical Aberration

Historically, however, the catalogue evolved prior to classification. In the pre-classification era, no classification (in the third sense described in section 13) existed, to which the main line of communication could allot a domain. The earlier form of the catalogue did not therefore become a domain of classification. The pattern of the catalogue got frozen and petrified, as it were, in that pre-classification shape and structure. It is proving difficult to break this rock of hardened catalogue-tradition and to tell the catalogue, as it were, "The main line of communication has assigned a domain for classification. Classification has reached an advanced stage in its evolution. It is high time that you, as a loop-line in comminication, become a second domain for classification to facilitate effective communica-cation." We are now passing through a difficult age when this historical aberration, in the evolution of the potential zone in the consumer's end of com-munication, is forming a serious obstruction in the path of progress. The irony here is that this obstruc-tion, due to conformity to out-moded tradition, finds its defender in a comparatively young community which has grown, during but three centuries, out of a nucleus of arch-non-conformists who risked everything to resist and escape the deadly grip of outmoded tra-dition elsewhere.

323 Third Domain of Classification

As regards increase in number and as the persons taking part in the intellectual team-work, needing their use, grows in number, a second loop-line has to be laid to make communication efficient and expeditious. The second loop-line is in relation to the domain ZT of the main line. It is in this loop-line that reference-librarians work. It is here that they meet the consumers, probe into their minds and help them, by trial and error, to enunciate their thought-needs in exact terms. As it has been explained in section 173, in this delicate human task characterised by all the surprises of emergent evolution, a structurally ex-pressive, analytico-synthetic classification is of im-mense help to the reference librarian. No doubt, innate flair can go a long way in this matter. But the number of men with such superior flair, which society can spare for reference service, does not prove sufficient for the task as a result of the increase in the number of records piled up at T and the number of classes into which they have to be sorted out, and on account of the progressively lower intellectual strata from which the workers in co-operative intellectual teams have to be drawn. It therefore becomes necessary to discipline reference librarians in the technique of classification and its application to the probing of consumer's mind. Thus reference service becomes a second loop-line in communication, where classification finds its third domain.

324 Jigsaw Puzzle

The situation arising in communication inherent in intellectual team-work reminds one of jigsaw puzzle. At P we have records embodying all sorts of thought-mass being piled up incessantly. At Z we have all sorts of consumers of varying mental ability and of varying differentiated and yet related interests, who have to be helped to enunciate their thought-needs. The right ones among the records at P have to be matched with the right ones among the consumers at Z. To secure this, preparation is necessary at both ends. Classification is the means employed in that preparation. The records at P are transformed into class numbers and fanned out at T in the apupa pattern. The minds of the consumers are probed with the same classification as the means and the thought-masses found to be needed are transformed into class numbers and brought to T to be matched to the class numbers on the records. Trial and error will still be needed for delicate adjustment within very small limits very much like the delicate skilled work involved in the " make-ready " stage in printing work. The transformation of records is done in the domain PT. It is done by the classifier. The transformation of thought-masses is done on the second loopline of communication alongside the domain ZT. It is done by the reference librarian.

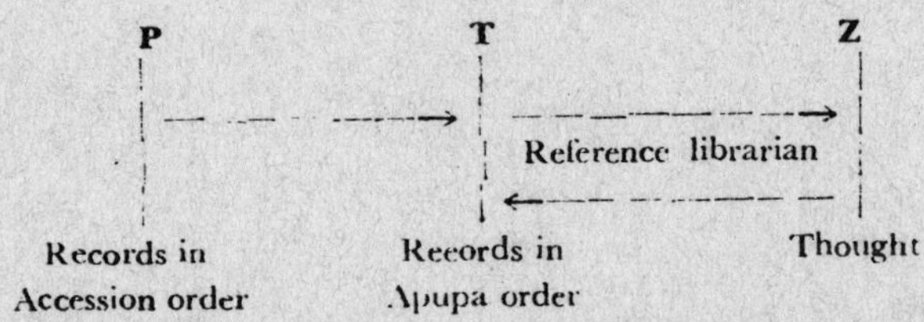

The help of the cataloguer also is taken on the loop-line of communication in the domain PT. The matching is done at T. This also is done by the reference librarian. The classifier who works in the domain PT and the reference librarian should work in frequent consultation with each other to make the matching perfect. The cataloguer who works in the loopline in the domain PT should also work in consultation with both of these. Then only the catalogue can be of maximum help in the first loop-line of communication alongside the domain ZT. The cataloguer's ideal should be to make the consumer pick out his records with the aid of the catalogue alone, without leaning on the reference librarian. This ideal may never be reached. But it must be approached as closely as possible. The need for the reference librarian to take the consumer into his loop-line should arise only when the thought-mass is very minute, very complicated in structure and also a newly created or unfamiliar one. For all familiar thought-mass which is simple in structure and large in content, the catalogue should prove sufficient for the jigsaw puzzle to be solved by the consumer all by himself.

325 Symbiosis

Classification will have a future as a means of communication and can retain its domain in communication, if and only if

(1) it keeps itself ever in step with formations of all sorts in the field of knowledge, which get transformed into records, so that the apupa pattern into which they are thrown is most helpful ;

(2) it keeps itself ever tested in its efficiency as a tool to probe into the minds of those who are engaged in intellectual teamwork of all sorts and to bring out the apupa pattern of their thought-needs ;

(3) unimpeded symbiosis is ever maintained between classification, catalogue and reference service so that the apupa patterns of the records and the expressed form of consumer's thought-needs match each other thoroughly.

3251 OUTMODED VIEW

If we persist in the view that classification is only an aid to shelf-arrangement and is conditioned by the physical set-up of the building in which the records are housed, there is nothing serious to be done. Classification will be an isolated affair without any organic connection with library catalogue or reference service. It may be continued purely as a local affair. It may even be an ever-transitory affair, altered from time to time. There will be nothing for the profession as a whole to deliberate upon either now or at any time. We can't speak of the future of classification.

3252 OUTMODED ASSUMPTION

If we still persist that any consumer, intelligent and able enough to be taken into an intellectual team-work, knows what he wants—knows the very records he wants—communication will not necessarily have use for classification. The records can be arranged alphabetically or by size or in accession order and be given mere press-marks. Learned workers would not need the services of a library profession to arrange their records. They could do it themselves. In fact they had been doing so till recently. But the Royal Society's Conference of 1948 regarded this as no longer practicable. It made it clear that the assumption was no longer valid. It recognised the need for technical assistance from the library profession to facilitate communication among the participants in intellectual team-work and in particular the need for classification effecting an everywhere-apupa pattern in the arrangement of records and of catalogue entries. The decision of the Library of the Surgeon-General's Office of U. S. A. to change the dictionary catalogue and provide a domain for classification in the catalogue is another testimony from a long-standing organisation set up for effective communication to aid intellectual team-work in a specific region of the field of knowledge.

3253 NEEDS OF REFERENCE SERVICE

But the need for assigning a domain for classification within the area of reference service is not yet clearly seen. Even the library profession does not seem to have clearly seen it. Perhaps the first explicit statement of it was formulated in my *Classification, coding and machinery for research* released by Unesco as document Unesco-NS-SL/3 on 30 June 1950.

326 Effect of Atomisation

The unprecedented atomisation of thought-mass being brought about by intellectual team-work has emphasised the need for invoking the aid of a faceted, phased, structurally expressive, analytico-synthetic classification in the area of reference service. The onslaught of atomisation threatened to break down communication even among persons engaged in the same piece of intellectual team-work. The etiology of this trouble was first wrongly attributed to the man in charge of the record not being a specialist in the region of the field of knowledge in which the intellectual team-work was being pursued. Subject-specialists were therefore put in charge of research-records, which are what records embodying atomised thought amount to. No doubt some relief did come by this remedy—but not full relief. This is because the correct etiology is not that the library staff did not have specialised knowledge but that its tool to facilitate communication—*viz.*, classification was not sharp enough to do the job. Once this is recognised, the need for research within the domain of classification in communication will be realised.

327 Effect of polyglotism

The unprecedented scatter, among diverse linguisitc regions of the earth, of the intellectual team-workers engaged on specific subjects has also emphasised the need for invoking the aid of a faceted, phased, structurally expressive, analytico-synthetic depth—classification in the area of search of relevant materials. Economy rules out translation of all the research-records on a specific subject into a single language and the cataloguing of them in that language. On the other hand if each research-record is classified, *i.e.*, if its soul is expressed in terms of class numbers and if the entries of all the records are assembled and arranged by the class numbers, the resulting apupa pattern will throw together all like records irrespective of their natural languages. If the same classification scheme is used universally, the classification of each record can be done in the country of its origin by classifiers who know its language. The classified entries coming from diverse countries can then be thrown into the apupa pattern mechanically with the aid of the class numbers and without the need to read and understand the languages of the record. The reference librarian can easily interpret the content of a record in foreign tongues, with the aid of their class numbers.

3271 ECONOMY IN TRANSLATION

The above procedure will lead to considerable economy in translation-service. If the class number is a fully expressive and individualising one, there will be no need to translate all the records or even to express their gist in the language of the country in order to enable the consumer to decide whether he will benefit by a close perusal of them. The class number would have by itself given the necessary help to the reader in deciding this issue. At any rate the number of records which need to be rendered into his own language can be considerably reduced. This will lead to much economy in translation-service. To carry this economy to the fullest extent, it is desirable that the classification of each research-record should be done in the country of origin *i.e.* by classifiers who know its language. Thus the domain of classification touches in its extereme even the domain of translation. The more thoroughly organised the domain of classification is, the smaller will be the actual domain for translation and hence the smaller will be the cost of translation service.

328 Domain at producer End

We have seen in the last two sections that to minimise the obstruction to communication set by diversity of natural languages, recourse can be had to a single artificial classificatory language. To make this effective three factors are necessary.

(1) The classificatory language should be truly universal *i.e.* it should be capable of expressing specific subjects peculiar to any culture whatever. It should not be biased in favour of any one cultural group.

(2) The same classificatory language should be adopted throughout the world.

(3) It should also be maintained without developing any dialetcs *i.e.* its development

should be such as to preserve its universality and sameness throughout the world.

This is not possible in a natural language as it grows in the mouth of the common man and its growth cannot therefore be controlled. But the artificial classificatory language grows in the hands of a few classifiers. While it is necessary to have classifiers in each linguistic region of the world, the group in each linguistic region should and can be reduced to a small size and the group can live and work together. The National Central Library of each country is the place for it. By this means and by providing for international consultation and conference among the various national groups of classifiers, the growth of classificatory language can be internationally controlled and maintained as a single non-splintering universal language. This means that classification should be done even at the producer's end. This means, in its turn, that the domain for classification should be shifted from the domain PT shown in section 3212 to the domain JK in the producer's end as shown below.

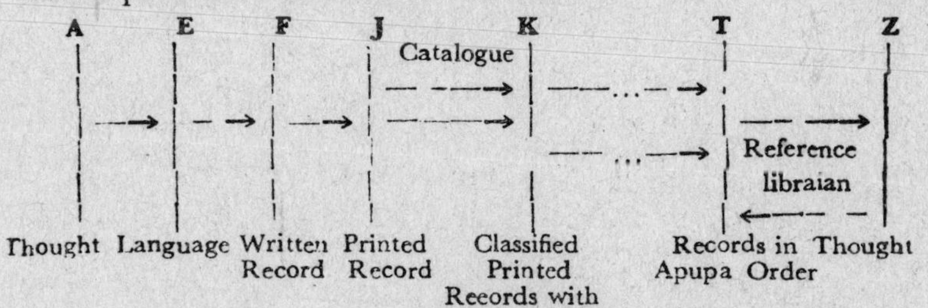

In the domain JK the transformer is the classifier and the means is classification.

3281 NATIONAL ECONOMY

In addition to the maintenance of purity in the

single classificatory language of the world, the shifting of the domain of classification to the producer's end and its centralisation will also lead to national economy. If 1,000 copies of a book or periodical are distributed by the publisher to 1,000 libraries and if the classification is done at the consumer's end, 1,000 persons will have to read them and classify them more or less at the same time. But if classification is centralised at the producer's end, only one person will be needed to do the work. The remaining 999 persons can be taken away from this repetitive work and turned on to the more human and vital work of reference service belonging to the domain represented by the loop-line ZT in section 324.

3282 PRE-NATAL CLASSIFICATION

A further step in the organisation at the producer's end can facilitate communication even more. Communication can be obstructed not only by language-hurdle but also by time-lag. Documentation—*i.e.* classification, cataloguing and abstracting—takes time. If time is taken to do it in the domain PT at consumer's end, a record ready for consumption in a nascent state is held up and denied access to consumers, leading to a legitimate protest from the Third Law. By shifting documentation to the domain JK at the producer's end, the same hold-up and time-lag will persist. Though the consumer may not be aware of it, the Third Law is and it does protest. Even this offence against Third Law can be avoided by shifting the domain of documentation to the domain FJ. In the case of books, a set of forme-proofs can be supplied to the National Central Library for documentation purposes. The classification, cataloguing and abstracting can be done before the preliminary pages are struck. The class number can be printed in the book and the catalogue cards can be released along with the book itself. In the case of articles in periodicals, either an extra-copy of the manuscript or a copy of the galley-proof can be sent to the National Central Library and the class number and the abstract can be prepared early enough to be printed with the article. Also, the documentation-entry for the abstracting periodical concerned can be produced even as the article is struck off. This I call ' Pre-natal Documentation ' which automatically implies ' Pre-natal Classification.'

CHAPTER 33

Time-and Space-Facets

This chapter and the four succeeding ones will be devoted to the manifestation of the five fundamental categories as facets and foci. In many specific subjects, time-and space-facets occur together. When they do so we have either local description or historical account. In classifying time it may be helpful to distinguish between public calendar, geological calendar and private calendar.

331 Public Time Focus

3311 After 1000 A. D.

It is usual to take the beginning of the Christian era as the origin. A decade may ordinarily be taken as a normal focus in the modern period *i.e.* the time-range falling after 1000 A. D. It may be contracted or sharpened to a year, month, day, etc. when required. The need for this may often arise in documentation work. It may have to be enlarged to a century in some specific subjects. A book like G. N. Clark's *Seventeenth century* for example does not admit of the time-focus being even as sharp as a decade. In the range " After 1000 A. D." speciation proceeds by discrete steps, the successive modular stages being century, decade, year, month, day, hour, etc. It is therefore convenient to denote a century by a single digit and derive numbers for decades, years, etc., by adding further digits to it.

3312 Between 1000 B. C. and 1000 A. D.

The time-range 1000 B. C. to 1000 A. D. is far removed from us. The materials dealing with this time-context may not warrant the use of even a decade as the normal focus. This is the effect of perspective. The century may be a more convenient normal focus. Of course this may have to be contracted to a decade, year etc. in certain cases and enlarged to a millennium in others. Thus within this range speciation may have to begin with millennium and so it may be helpful to denote a millennium by a single digit. Of course to denote a century in the A. D. subrange we may have to add a century-digit after the millennium-digit, and so also for a decade, a year, etc. In the BC range the "Method of Complement" should be used, in arriving at the century-digit, decade-digit etc. to be added after the millennium digit. This means that the century-digit to be added should be the difference between 9 and the number standing for the B. C. century. This is necessary because the class number is uni-directional, the direction being the same as the one we find in the A. D. range. But in the normal method of reckoning, the B. C. years run in the opposite direction. The failure to recognise this is a cause of inconvenience in the Universal Decimal Classification. But the Colon Classification has implemented this.

3313 BETWEEN 10,000 AND 1,000 B.C.

The range 10,000 to 1,000 B. C. is nearly prehistoric. However, we have to recognise this range and provide for its division, since dated materials belonging to this time-context are already available though meagrely, as a result of Egyptian and Mohenjo-Daro excavations. As this range is B. C., the Method of Complement should be used to derive the digits for a millennium, century, etc.

332 Geological Time Focus

It is doubtful if historical records belonging to the time-context "Before 10,000 B. C." will ever become available. Even a millennium will be too small for use as unit of time in that far-off age. Perhaps an appropriate unit will be the geological one determined by stratigraphy like Eozoic, Palaeozoic, Mesozoic, Eailnozoic, and Quarternary.

333 Private Time Focus

In documentation work, time-measure by public calendar may prove to be unhelpful in certain specific subjects. The only relevant time-measure will have to be from an origin determined by the specific subject itself—according to its private calendar so to speak. There should be a notational device to distinguish the three kinds of time-foci, *viz*., public, geological and private. A model has been suggested in the *Abgila*. In the case of private time focus the unit of time may cover a vast range from micro-second to beyond a millennium. It may be helpful to devise a set of signature digits to indicate the unit in use. It may also be necessary to have a notational device to indicate periodicity.

334 Methodology

We are now in a position to examine the features of the methodology used. Time is one-dimensional, using "dimension" in the sense in which we say that a geographical area is two-dimensional. It is the simplest fundamental category and reveals the methodology with the least complexity. Though time may be a continuum, we derive its divisions by breaking it into discrete intervals. The extent of all the unit-intervals is not the same. It varies with the range where it is used. The unit-intervals chosen are merely conventional and are not determined by any compelling units. A non-conformist specific subject will stretch itself over a time-interval overlapping two or more of the normal units. It is necessary to have a notational device to indicate such an overlapping focus. The *Abgila* has suggested the use of forward arrow (→) and backward arrow (←) to denote an overlapping focus. The arrow is to connect the end-points. The two kinds of arrows are to be used according as the movement is towards the future or towards the past.

335 Space-Facet

The fundamental category ' space ' often occurs as geographical facet or focus. Unlike time, earth is finite and two-dimensional. There is no conventional origin that we can adopt. The normal focus also is not to be fixed by convention. It cannot therefore be uniform even within small areas. It is in fact pre-determined by physiographical, political, administrative and other factors. Its extent will vary from class to class. Classification has to accept all this as it occurs. What is more inconvenient is that these units will not satisfy the Canon of Permanence. This creates a notational difficulty which appears to be partially insoluble ; with the result, there appears to be no alternative to having several sequences, say corresponding to the different epochs of historical geography. The Decimal Classification gives two schedules—one for the Ancient World and the other for the Modern World. But this dichotomy is far from sufficient to meet the political vicissitudes of the world.

336 World

The world as a whole figures in many specific subjects, and so it must be represented by a digit. The earth's surface may have to be divided on the basis of several trains of characteristics. There are divisions due to land and water-formations—continents and oceans. There are also political divisions whose boundaries change not infrequently as it has happened in Eastern Europe after the First World War and in the Indian sub-continent on 15 August 1947. The earth's surface may have to be divided also on the basis of political alliance of varying degrees of affinity between several sovereign nations like the United Nations and the Commonwealth of today and the Roman Empire, the League of Nations and the British Empire of the past. It may also have to be divided on the basis of language, religion, political ideology and in fact on the basis of any subject whatever. Classification should provide for all these contingencies. The Colon Classification uses the facile subject-device for this purpose. But the use of this device presents some difficulties which need solution. The earth's surface may also have to be divided into the conventional climatic zones and hemispheres and even on the basis of latitude and longitude. Air-navigation is introducing the formation of new zones of a different kind. These too must be provided for.

337 Countries

Countries which are sovereign political units will have to be divided on the basis of administrative characteristic also, in addition to most of the characteristics mentioned in section 336. The administrative divisions of a country flout the Canon of Permanence even more than the political divisions of the world. The *Abgila* has suggested an effective way of meeting the situation by the use of signature digits denoting the administrative characteristic and these being read with the foci in the time-facet. This problem requires further study.

338 Diverse Groupings and Localities

Documentation will often require the individualisation of localities, of isolated areas and formations like cities, deserts, mountains, peaks, valleys, rivers, lakes, gulfs, capes and so on. It will also require classes of contiguity like Eastern Districts, Far East, Near East, South East Asia, and Pacific Countries. There may be need for orientation-divisions in relation to any area. There may be need also for dichotomic divisions like " Outside Asia," " Dollar Area " and " Outside of Dollar Area," " Communistic Countries " and "Non-communistic Countries" and so on. Space outside earth may have to be divided in diverse ways. Tiny local spaces too may have to be divided. Notation should be organically designed to take care of all these diverse demands of documentation without day-to-day dependence on the classificationist. In documentation work we have often to deal with surprise classes which arise and become dominant for the moment. Without a high degree of autonomy, classifiers will not be able to organise nascent materials involving unexpected and even temporary foci in the space-facet.

CHAPTER 34

Preliminary Schedules

The chronological and the geographical schedules implied in chapter 33 will be in frequent demand in several specific subjects. It is therefore usual to give them as preliminary schedules at the very beginning of a classification scheme for convenience of reference. But these do not exhaust the preliminary schedules which should be given.

341 Linguistic Schedules

The language-schedule also will be in demand in more than one connection. It will be certainly needed in the main classes, literature and linguistics. As greater convenience will be had if the reading materials on a given specific subject are grouped by their languages, language-schedule will also be in demand in the construction of book numbers. The Colon Classification and the Universal Decimal Classification include linguistic schedules among their preliminary schedules. These schedules require careful scrutiny so that they may be reconstructed in conformity to established degrees of linguistic affinity. The Universal Decimal Classification being based on the Decimal Classification as its core is handicapped in this matter. Languages belonging to the same family stand separated by languages of foreign families coming in between them. The Colon Classification avoids this to a considerable extent. However, there is need to tidy up some of the sub-divisions of the three major families, *viz.*, Indo-Germanic, Semetic, and Dravidian families, and to see if detailed schedules for the languages outside these families can be better constructed than by the geographical device used by the Colon Classification.

342 Common Sub-divisions

Another commonly occurring preliminary schedule is that of so called "Common Sub-divisions." this schedule requires drastic purging because it happens to be a hotch-potch. Its divisions are not based on the same characteristic. Some of the divisions are based on the literary form of exposition like verse, drama, fiction, lecture, picture, etc. Certain others are based on the mode of arrangement of entries within reference books like,systematic, numerical, alphabetical, chronological and so on. Some others are based on kinds of reference books like bibliography, atlas, statistics, history, biography, collected works and so on. Again some of the common sub-divisions like bibliography, biogrphy and syllabus are best placed anterior to the classes subdivided by them. Others like institutions are better placed posterior to them. In the Universal Decimal Classification the common sub-divisions are based even on physical features like pamphlets, gramophone records, sound films, microfilms, etc.

343 A Suggestion

It has been suggested in the *Abgila* that it is desirable to break up the schedule of the traditional common sub-divisions into three groups relating respectively to the thought-content, the language and form of exposition, and the nature, size, shape, etc. of the reading material viewed as physical commodity. Indeed it has been shown that help can be taken in this matter from a traditional analysis well stabilised since ancient times. Though the substance behind this tradition may not be accepted by moderns who would deny concepts not reduceable ultimately to sense perception, the scheme furnished by the tradition is of help in analysis in various contexts. According to this tradition, every individual has

(1) *Atman* (Soul) ;

(2) *Sukshma Sarira* (Subtle or intangible, or astral body) ; and

(3) *Sthula Sarira* (Gross, or tangible or sensually perceptible body).

Applying this tradition to reading and kindred materials, we get the following equivalents :

Soul	= Thought-content	= Specific subject	= Class Number
Subtle body	= Medium of expression embodying the thought	= Language and form of exposition	= Book Number
Gross body	= Physique embodying the expressed thought	= Nature, size, shape, etc., of the reading and kindred materials viewed as physical commodities.	= Sequence Number

The common sub-divisions based on thought-content should become part of class-numbers. Those based on the language and form of exposition should go

Aith the book-numbers and not with the class-num bers. The common sub-divisions based on the physical nature of the reading materials should go with what has been called Sequence-Number in my *Library administration* (1935) and not with class-numbers or book-numbers.

344 Problems for Investigation

Whether the above analysis is accepted or not, there is no doubt that the traditional schedule of common sub-divisions should be drastically re-examined. Moreover many of the common sub-divisions are in need of being fitted with facets if they are to have individualising quality and be fit for the depth-classification needed by documentation. Unfortunately we do not have much material for comparative study in this matter, as the Colon Classification is the only one that has so far systematically fitted common sub-divisions with facets. The facet-analysis of common sub-divisions, I expect, will bring up several points for investigation.

345 Institutions

Among the posterior common sub-divisions, institutions form a very important category in documentation work. As an institution is a social organisation, its facets are bound to be many and its foci will demand varying degrees of sharpening. Documentation work in social sciences cannot be effective until we are able to iron out the difficulties connected with the common sub-division of ' Institutions.' The Universal Decimal Classification has worked out some divisions under the generalia class ' Institution.' No doubt these divisions can be attached to any class number by the Colon Device of the Universal Decimal Classification. But the schedules for institutions do not group the foci into homogeneous facets nor do they sharpen the foci adequately and isolate them ; with the result, several topics cannot be individualised. Investigation of this problem has just been taken on hand and the findings are likely to be given in the *Abgila* for September 1951.

CHAPTER 35

Energy-Facet

Energy is perhaps the most ubiquitous of all the fundamental categories. Indeed there can be no basic class without an energy-facet. Moreover many specific subjects—particularly at the deep level of documentation— call for several energy-facets. It is conjectured that the several energy-facets of a specific subject will generally form a chain of successively dependant facets. Whether this conjecture is true can be verified only by examining the problem-facets in as many different subjects as possible. As the current practice is not explicitly or consciously using the facet-idea and at any rate not using the facet-terminology, the subject-headings of the various industrial subjects, which have been worked out *ad hoc* in different industries in several countries, should be collected and collated by a kind of what may be called fractional distillation which should be able to separate out the terms in the subject-headings which belong to energy-facets. It is in some such way that an investigation of energy-facets can be initiated.

352 Mnemonics and Primordial Schedules

The idea of unscheduled mnemonics developed in the Colon Classification is likely to be of help in reducing the number of primordial energy-facets. For something common lies veiled behind the varied multiplicity of phenomena. The unscheduled mnemonics really plant themselves on this veiled commonness. When arranged according to these mnemonics the problem-foci are likely to fall in a helpful order in most subjects. If all the parallel or analogous meanings of each Arabic numeral could be listed, a few primordial schedules can be made easily applicable to different specific subjects. This is a piece of work which awaits to be done. It can be done only as the work referred to in the preceding sections progresses or perhaps even gets completed. In spite of this, the number of primordial schedules is likely to be greatest for the manifestation of the fundamental category energy. This is so because the number of ways of manipulating things is of a much higher order than the number of things themselves I am not able to guess at present how the primordial energy schedule can be designed. I have every hope that when the work referred to above gets done, sufficient suggestion will come for ward in regard to signature digits.

353 Potency of Energy-Facets

The efficiency of a scheme of classification and its expectation of life will be determined largely by its capacity to isolate, handle and organise energy-facets in different subjects. For it is energy which enlivens matter. It is matter enlivened by energy which leaves its trail in space-time. It is only when energy-facets develop that personality gets differentiated and becomes comprehensible. Such is the potency of energy-facets. This is all in keeping with Vedic and other mystic traditions. Shri Aurobindo has described it in several of his writings. The Trinity consists of *Purusha* (=the divine personality unmanifest), *Prakriti* (=the inert matter in need of enrichment by *Purusha*) and *Sakti* (=the energy-principle needed to effect the enrichment). The phenomenal world owes its existence to the functioning of the energy-principle. Intellectual pursuits are largely concerned with the phenomenal world. Helpful organisation of the result of intellectual pursuits and particularly their records should naturally depend on the efficiency with which the energy-facets and the foci in them are isolated and arranged in a helpful order. The *Bija Aksharas* (=Seminal letters) of the Indian tradition may throw light on this problem if we could get at their esoteric significance. I have been seeking it. But I have not yet met with success.

CHAPTER 36

Matter-Facet

Matter-Facet is not likely to present as many difficulties as energy-facet. However, we have to recognise different levels of manifestation of the fundamental category matter:—matter *qua* matter, substance, commodity, artificial commodities, and prefabricated commodities.

361 Matter *qua* Matter

In the first place we have to recognise undifferentiated matter *i.e.*, matter not distinguished as different substances like iron, silver, gold, etc. Physics is the main class which is concerned with the bare matter *qua* matter. In physics we may have the need to have matter-facets based upon various physical properties as characteristics. There is, for example, the state-of-matter characteristic. Solids, liquids and gases are the commonly known foci in that facet. But we can have several other foci ; for example, between the solid and the liquid states, the surface-state has been recognised as a possible state of matter, though the study of it came out first under the misleading title *Chemistry of surfaces.* Between liquid and gaseous states there may be similarly some other intermediary state. Beyond the gaseous state we have the molecular state (*vide* molecular rays), ionised state and the whole group of disintegrated states known as fundamental particles. There may also be need to build matter-schedules based upon the measure in which several physical properties like density, elasticity, specific heat, refractive index, dielectric constant, magnetic permeability, etc. are incident. Modern industrial chemistry needs matter classified on the basis of all such characteristics. Documentation work has therefore to depend upon matter-schedules based on the measure of such physical constants.

362 Substance

By substance we mean matter differentiated on the basis of a complex of physical and chemical properties. The simplest category of substances is that of the inorganic elements in chemistry. Several schemes exist for arranging the elements in a helpful order. Decimal order, Gmelin's order, Colon order, and arrangement by atomic numbers. All of these develop difficulties when used in constructing numbers for compounds. The difficulties become overpowering when we enter the realm of organic and bio-substances. A satisfactory scheme of classification for natural substances is yet to be devised.

363 Commodities

By commodities we mean substances reduced to a consumable or a serviceable form. We can have various stages in it giving rise to semi-commodities, and ultimate commodities. Here matter is divided essentially on the basis of utility characteristic. Commodities may be of technological or geological or of botanical or animal origin. In fact all manufactures and agricultural and animal produces come under the category of commodities. No doubt the subject-device will go a long way in arranging commodities according to the canon of mnemonics. But this may not prove sufficient. As we have stated in section 2351, about a million commodities have been listed by the world of commerce. Considerable work awaits to be done in constructing suitable primordial schedules of commodities. Each specific subject may have its own favoured commodities. It will be necessary to arrange them by the Favoured Category Device. Over and above this it may also have to use other commodities. To suit this situation it will be desirable to have all the commodities arranged in different primordial schedules with distinctive signature digits. The number of such primordial schedules needed is not yet known. Whether 20 or 40 or 400 will be sufficient will have to be determined by examining the schedules or the subject headings in actual use in different industries.

364 Artificial Substances

Modern technological progress has added to the difficulties of classification by competing with nature in producing artificial substances and semi-commodities as substitutes for natural ones. The range and the grades of these artificial substances are far greater than those of natural commodities. We do not have enough experience of them as yet to enable us to enunciate any basis for constructing helpful schedules of them. This difficulty is increased by the fact that their true genesis and composition are not always disclosed. The urge for trade-secrecy leads their inventors and manufacturers to give them fanciful names which amount almost to proper names. This drives us often to invoke the help of alphabetical device in constructing schedules of such artificial commodities. This really amounts giving up true classificaton.

365 Prefabricated Commodities

Another development in the manifestation of matter is the production of prefabricated commodities. Prefabrication is taken to varying stages. This phenomenon is too recent—and at any rate it is so in Indian experience—to allow us to hazard any suggestion for the construction of helpful schedules to classify them.

CHAPTER 37

Personality-Facet

It has been already stated in section 1374 that all the other facets are but attributes of the personality-facet. It may be even said that each basic class is a super-personality. The super-personality may have other personality-facets. Even in rough classification, personality-facet is more likely to be represented than any other facet. Moreover the foci in personality-facets may have to be derived on the basis of time, space, matter and subject characteristics. Still they are personality-facets and not time-facets etc.

371 Person

The personality-facet may be formed on the basis of types or groups of persons. In the Colon Classification they are called entity facet in psychology and education, and group facet in sociology. In medicine the human body is the super-personality and its regional and functional parts and their parts constitute its personality-facets. In botany and zoology, plant and animal bodies have a similar position. In agriculture and animal-husbandry crops and useful animals constitute the super-personality and their species and strains, and the parts of their bodies may figure as personality-facets.

372 Material

In chemistry, technology and several of the useful arts, the fundamental category personality manifests itself as materials like substances, intermediate commodities and ultimate commodities. In subjects dealing with commodities, documentation work may have to recognise the fundamental category personality in several levels. It is best illustrated by an example. Let us take documentation work on bicycles which we shall take to be the super-personality in this context. The next level of manifestation of personality may have foci which relate to the make or the stamp like Hercules, Hind, and Raleigh, the power used like muscular and motor, and also the nature of the users like children's cycles, ladies' cycles and so on. All these three groups of facets involve the whole bicycle. We shall say that they belong to the first-order-level of personality. It is found that the three sub-levels in the first-order-level may be accommodated either as separate facets or as different groups in the same facet or in different octaves in the first-order array of one and the same facet. In the case of the cycle the last alternative is the most economical. This can be proved. We have to establish criteria to decide which of these alternatives is most appropriaate in any given subject. At the second-order-level, personality may manifest itself as foci constituting the parts recognisable in the cycle at first sight as the structural landmarks. These foci may be formed and arranged either by the principle of spatial contiguity or on the basis of function like wheels, frame, seat, gear, etc. At the third-order-level, personality may manifest itself as foci constituting the more detailed parts of each of the parts of the cycle—the structual landmarks in the part. This can be continued to levels of as many orders as necessary. Prior to a part being divided on the basis of its own parts, it may have to be divided as whole according to the make. Work along these lines has just begun. After applying this procedure to a large number of commodities, it may be possible to arrive at certain simple abstract principles by which personality facets and foci could be recognised and represented by classifiers without reference to the classificationist.

373 Geographical Area

In history and law, the fundamental category personality manifests itself as community. In history a community is usually represented by the geographical area occupied by it—a country or groups of countries or a district or a city or a village or any combinations of these. In law too a community may be represented by a geographical area. This is without prejudice to the fact that in some cases it may also be a religious group or a group based on any other factor. In that case personality will manifest itself as the foci of the class 'religion.'

374 Chronological Epoch

In biography the fundamental category personality may manifest itself as a chronological epoch, say a year or a decade. It is so in the Colon Classification where a biographee is represented by the year of his birth. In literature too, the Colon Classification represents an author as a time-focus.

375 Languages

In linguistics and literature the first order manifestation of personality is in the form of languages. In linguistics there may be further manifestations of the fundamental category personality in the form of stages of language like Anglo-Saxon, Middle English and Modern English and variants of language like dialect, slang and jargon.

376 Common Sub-divisions

It has been stated in Chapter 34 that many of the common sub-divisions need to be fitted with facets. The object of so fitting them with facet is really to individualise the entities like institutions, periodicals and biographies. In fact these are to be regarded as manifestations of personality. It is found that geographical and chronological devices together serve the purpose of individualising them. It may not therefore be inappropriate to view facets and foci attached to such common sub-divisions as manifestations of personality.

377 Literature

In the main class literature we get the furthest reach of personality. Here the highly evolved, fully differentiated, unique personality of an author has to be represented through the combined manifestations of the fundamental category personality in the three facets, *viz.*, language, form and time. The even subtler personality of a literary piece needs the services of these three, and to their combination another manifestation of personality called work-facet has to be added to get it fully expressed. The Colon Classification has done so.

CHAPTER 38

Research and Organisation

We are now in a position to have a peep into the future of classification. Classification originally began to help arrangement of books in a library. But as we have seen in the earlier chapters its use has now been extended to the featuring of articles in periodicals in a helpful way in documentation lists. In this use it has to handle micro-units of thought. Another use for classification has been shown to be probing into the minds of thinkers and pulling out the apupa pattern of their ways of thinking. Here the units of thought to be individualised become even smaller. Wht is more, their tiny extent presents many more phases and facets than macro-units of thought embodied in books. We have thus transformed the concept of classification. The chief question that matters for our decision in accepting or rejecting a certain concept is whether or not we expect fruitful results from the use of that concept irrespective of earlier uses of it. The question therefore is : Is the new concept of classification worthwhile ? Will classificatory language with such a purpose lead to fruitful results ? Since the development of classificatory language is still in its very beginning it is too early to give a well-founded answer. But I have a feeling that it may be of more than accidental help to world-communication and understanding, and will supply the very basis of it. However, the way in which the Colon Classification is constructed and the new type of foundations on which it is built need not be the most appropriate for the purpose. This was only a first attempt, so to speak : or perhaps the second since the Universal Decimal Classification can be taken to have been the first. The Universal Decimal Classification did not go the whole hog in redesigning the foundation of classification. Twenty-five years of experiment with the Colon Classification has demonstrated the possible advantages of a drastic re-design of foundations. To my mind it has also demonstrated the need for it.

381 Change of Foundation

Periods of rapid and extensive development of a discipline are frequently periods of loose thinking about its foundations. The recognition of the need for a catastrophic change of the foundation emerges rather slowly. Such was the case with mathematics in the eighteenth century and with biology in the nineteenth. So it is today with classification at the levels of idea and notation alike. With a sort of perverse professional modesty, many evade facing the problem by insisting that they classiy only in relation to the particular set-up of their respective libraries without too intimate a reference to the happenings in the field of knowledge either in the superficies or at varying depths. Inertia sometimes gets veneered with cleverness and makes the less modest bluff that to make people read is the essence and it mattered little how classification was done. Reflection shows however that classification has to be cared for seriously just to secure the essential purpose of facilitating communication among intellectual peers and of helping readers to get what they need unerringly, exhaustively and without loss of time. Reflection shows also that the levels of idea and notation can not be separated, or developed and enumerated independently of each other. Reflection shows further that if classification were merely manipulation of symbols, it would be as devoid of significance and utility as card play or chess. There can then be no talk of serious research or organisation for it. But it is now known that classification has an important part to play in international communication and intellectual teamwork and the levels of idea and notation are inseperable in the designing of classification.

382 Need for Numbers

Classification can illumine the field of knowledge. It can even be prohpetic. To make it fit for this new role, it must be placed on a new type of foundation and built in a new way. This calls for considerable research. Communication of thought has to depend on helpful arrangement and selection. Whatever be the psychology of the arranging and selecting process, this process is facilitated by the use of artificial counters or symbols which represent only the general factors figuring in the arrangement and selection and not any which is too specific for the purpose and which may and should therefore be excluded. Class numbers imply as much purposive abstraction as mathematical symbols or the symbols of formal logic. And yet while calculus or a system of symbolic representation is a convenience but not a necessity for the reasoning process, it is a necessity for the process of apupa arrangement of specific subjects and the precise formulation of one's subject-needs in an apupa pattern.

It is as impossible to feature nascent thought in a helpful order without class numbers, as it is to carry on modern trade without cheques or book-credits or to build modern bridges without special tools. It is the overwhelming volume quantity, quality, intension, and speed of formation of new thought which call for the aid in all these cases. One of the important features of to-day is that many nations are reviving and becoming creative. Rate of production of new thought has increased a hundred-fold. The growing improvement in higher education everywhere has fortunately made it impossible to print books and periodicals on scientific and industrial matters in several languages spoken by comparatively small nations and being revived into effective media for transfer of subtle and specialised thought. But what is of benefit to these countries themselves may in some cases be detrimental to the world at large and even to authors and thinkers in so far as thoughts which deserved diffusion all over the world are now made accessible merely to a small fraction that should be interested in them. We thus get into trouble. It is when we get into trouble that thinking begins. In this case thinking has taken us to documentation and documentation has taken us to depth-classification demanding expressive analytico-synthetic class numbers.

383 Need for Empiricism

Viewed linguistically, class numbers may be said to be descriptive epigrams made of substantives and conjunctions alone. Viewed psychologically, they may be said to be abstractions. Viewed logically they may be said to be empirical. Viewed metaphysically, they are creatures of pragmatism. These supplementary modes of approach are not usually exclusive. Classificationists should be materialistic rather than mathematical. They should not excel in grasping some fruitful idea and elaborating it with such a perfection and finality of form that humanity is compelled, through sheer admiration, to strain the specific subjects to make them fit these perfect forms. They should on the other hand be more eager to observe the actual helpful orders among specific subjects from the point of the frequency of the seekers and design the classification to preserve those orders. They should love individualisaition and helpfulness more than elegance. They should adopt the Darwinian method of empricism.

3831 METHOD OF WORK

Empirical approach implies observation of the diverse ways in which new specific subjects are formed and the field of knowledge is atomised in commercial houses, production plants, industrial laboratories, institutes for fundamental research, fields of social studies and academic cloisters. The opportunity to visit industrial plants and laboratories in the U.S.A. last summer gave me a new insight into the problem of designing classification. As a follow-up work, the entries in the abstracting periodicals should be examined, grouped, tabulated and statistically studied in order to isolate all the modes of formation of new specific subjects particularly the specialised ones of minute extension. Librametry will have to develop new techniques to do this job.

3832 SOCIAL PRESSURE

Puranik's paper *Field of knowledge and its repurcussions on classification* in the 1951 March issue of the *Abgila* is significant in this connection. The progressive elaboration of the notational technique and the forging of new techniques are seen to be the result, not of mere academic exercises, but of unmistakable happenings in the field of knowledge which have created a social necessity and pressure. His findings can be seen from the following diagram showing the shift in the frequency of three modes of formation of specific subjects.

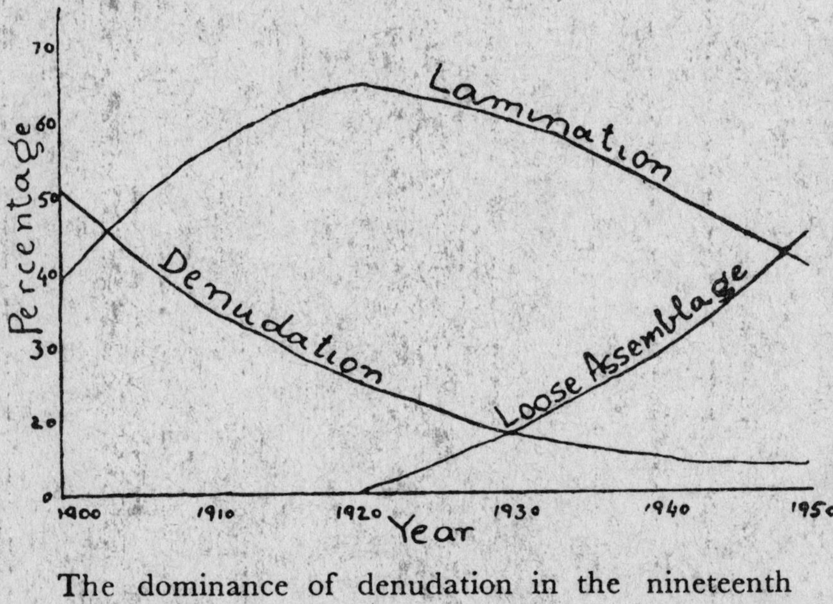

The dominance of denudation in the nineteenth century explains the Decimal Classification basing itself almost solely on decimal fraction-notation. The relative dominance of lamination and the going down of denudation at the end of the first quarter of the Twentieth century explains the Colon Classification having introduced facet-notation. The joint dominance of loose assemblage and lamination today—in the middle of the nineteenth century—explains the feeling of discomfort and despair in the world of classification. It shows that the call for research into the foundations of classification is based on social necessity.

3833 Strict Parallelism

All empirical world is made up of inter-related parts. This means that it has structure whose parts involve relation, *i.e.*, order. This decides that classificatory language should be an ordinal language. We must first study the order in the empirical world and build our classificatory language in a similar order instead of thrusting on the world the primitive structure of enumerative classification. The empirical search for world-structure and the building of class numbers of similar structure is what an expressive analytico-synthetic classification does. Its foundation has to be different from that of enumerative classification.

384 Semiotic of Classification

When the foundations of mathematics came to be redesigned, they landed themselves first in symbolic logic. When it was fully realised that both mathematics and symbolic logic were artificial languages designed for a particular purpose, the importance of their semiotic was realised. It is only after this was realised that it was possible to build true foundations. We have something to learn from this. If we realise that classification is an artificial language designed for a particular purpose, the surest way of designing its foundations will have to pass through the semiotic of classification. This is a new terrain. All that we can now say about it is that the syntactical rules of a classificatory language will have only Formation Rules but no Transformation Rules; because in classification we do not derive sentences from sentences. We concentrate only on the ordinary, grammatical structure of language. In other words, classificatory syntax will be quite different from logical syntax. With regard to its semantics our objective should be to establish multi-ordinal terms (unscheduled mnemonics) which will acquire a differing and unique meaning in each Gestalt. Research in this region will have to begin from the very alpha and beta.

385 Need for Terminology

Any branch of science, which is not stationary but progressive, must from time to time renew or revise its terminology. New terms must be formed not only for newly discovered ideas but also for new ideas resulting from new ways of considering old facts. Traditional terms often cramp the minds of investigators and may form a hindrance to fertile developments. I think that one of the first steps to be taken is to establish an effective terminology for developing thought in classification. When the area for investigation is itself a language-system, as it is the case with classification, one of the first steps to be taken is to establish the necessary new terminology in the meta-language to facilitate precise thinking about the object-language. The optical terminology described in section 1517 is only a sample. As research in the object-language of classification proceeds, the terminology in the metalanguage will evolve naturally.

386 Resistance

People outside the profession cannot believe that we are serious when we talk of research in classification. For it has no meaning to them. In fact, any serious work in abstract thought cannot have meaning to many.

3861 RESISTANCE TO TOIL

But a more serious resistance comes from a section of the library profession itself. Its prejudice against careful classification and research in the discipline of classification is part of the human impatience with technique. It arises from the fact that men are interested in results and would like to attain them without the painful toil which is the essence of our mortal finitude. It is time that the library profession gets over such a prejudice Much international effort is now being wasted in building on faulty foundations. The earlier we gird up our loins and face the problem of foundation the better it will be. Every year's evasion of this very difficult but very essential task means not only ineffectiveness in the result but also adding to the load of the coming generation. The so-called Principle of Starvation and arbitrary diversion of starved digits cannot lead to any consistent result. The library profession should shake off the despair which threatens to descend on it and be manly enough to face the field of knowledge squarely and develop a classification which can keep step with it.

3862 Resistance to Change

One of the objections commonly raised against change of classification is the cost of re-classifying old stock. This position is untenable since it would logically imply that all future should be tied up eternally to some past year when the scheme of classification in use was designed. No technological plant of the past is thus given the right to block the way to all progress, in the world of industry and indeed in any sphere of life. Library classification can not be an exception if it is to survive and not stultify itself. Whatever the cost is, revision must be undertaken.

38621 Osmotic Revision

The cost of revision need not be great. A cheap and sufficiently effective procedure will be as follows:

(1) Fix a definite date on and after which the new classificatory language is to be brought into use;

(2) Classify by that scheme all the new materials that arrive on and after that date;

(3) Have a conversion table to change from one scheme to another, so that relevant old materials might be picked up without undue delay;

(4) Reclassify any old material, that is called for use, by the new scheme and absorb it in the new sequence;

(5) Spot out regions of the old sequence which are in greater demand and reclassify and absorb that region in the new sequence even in anticipation of demand; and

(6) Work out and carry out a programme of priority in this manner to reclassify the old sequence.

It is likely that some materials of the old sequence may be too dead to deserve re-classification. Generally if the scheme in use had been of a sufficiently high potency, the need for change to one of higher potency will arise only if a drastic realignment is called for by major revolutionary formations in the field of knowledge in exceptional epochs of turbulance in the world of thought. In such an event, a good deal of older materials will be outmoded and become dead materials. The demand for them will be only too few and far between to justify re-classification and even then only for antiquarian work by a spare few. These few can be helped with the conversion table. The result may be that a library and a documentation file, many centuries old, will be in two or more sequences corresponding to the numbers of knowledge-epochs, so to speak, through which it had per- sisted to exist. This I call Osmotic Revision.

3863 PROPHYLACTIC

If the resistance is melted, the re-designing of the classification should be such as to prevent occasion for the development of resistance. A prophylactic is called for. This can be ensured if we remember that to the evolution of the field of knowledge should correspond an evolution of classification. The Decimal Classification met this demand partially. This partial fulfilment has proved as dangerous as " little knowledge." The Universal Decimal Classification too has landed itself in partial fulfilment of the principle in the measure of its self-stultifying dependence, upon the Decimal Classification. A cent per cent fulfilment of the principle will lead to what I have called in the *Journal of documentation* (1949), a self-perpetuating classification which can face any challenge whatever of the field of knowledge. If such a self-perpetuating classification is designed, there will be nothing against which resistance can develop. To fulfill this a complete and radical rebuilding of the foundation of classification and of classificatory procedure is necessary. Such a revision will be laborious. A single man could not accomplish it in all its details. It will need prolonged team-work unified by the formulation of some fundamental concepts. Phase-and facet-analysis, an assortment of digits charged with ordinal values, suited to serve as substantives and conjunctions of all sorts and invested with multi-ordinal meanings called unscheduled mnemonics, and primordial schedules corresponding to the fundamental categories, which mark an extreme order of abstraction, constitute one possible set of such concepts. Other sets, even more powerful, may be evolved in due course. To work with such a set of fundamental concepts and to evolve even more productive ones, the co-operation of several types of persons, of different nations and of several international organisations will be necessary.

387 Personnel for Work

The team of workers needed to examine the foundation of classification, redesign it if necessary, and maintain it in good repair will have to consist of five parties:

(1) The intuitive classificationist;
(2) The intellectual classificationist;
(3) The classifier;
(4) The reference librarian; and
(5) The workers in the different formations of the field of knowledge.

The division of labour among them may have to be somewhat as follows: The work of designing subdigits for the base to serve all possible needs of substantives and connectives, of isolating new phases, and prior to everything else visualizing the classificatory language as a whole and laying down its pattern by examples and rules and forging its notational apparatus so as to endow it with as great a potency as possible—these three fall to the share of the intuitive classificationist. The work of mnemonically fixing the numbers for the new classes which may appear from time to time demanding the extension of either an array or a chain, of finding by trial and error the facets of new subjects as and when the writings on them demand it, and deciding the order in which they should be assembled and of building up a dynamic science of classification—these three fall to the share of the intellectual classificationist. The work of translating the names of specific subjects, which appear before him embodied in books or articles, into the classificatory language and of bringing to the notice of the classificationist new specific subjects which baffle the existing notational apparatus, the scheduled foci, facet-formulae, and phase-formulae,—these two fall to the share of the classifier. The work of observing the faults and shortcomings of the classificatory language as disclosed in the glow of the triple contact between the reference librarian, the readers and the reading materials, and their documentation,—this falls to the share of the reference librarian. The work of isolating, enunciating in a natural language, and indicating the most helpful order of the myriads of specific subjects which take shape from time to time in the region of the field of knowledge in which he specializes—this falls to the share of the worker who is engaged in research. This analysis should not be taken in a ruthless and mechanical manner. This analyses the processes involved in the creation, maintenance and use of an artificial classificatory language of ordinal numbers rather than grouping the men who do the work. In exceptional cases, one and the same person may have the gift to play more than one role. All that this analysis emphasizes is that the rules of the game are different in the different processes. Many mistakes happen by the wrong man taking up the wrong job either under the lure of a false sense of prestige or under the maddening pressure of academic or political influence or under the tyranny of the ignorance of the demand of holism that any work is done best if it is shared willingly among several workers or classes of workers on a functional basis in the measure of their respective inborn and cultivated capacities, without attaching any differentiated and unequal monetary or prestige value to any share of the work.

388 Organisation

There appears to be no need to give up classification in despair. There is every chance that a scheme with a fairly long expectation of life can be designed if a proper organisation can be set up. The problem is too complicated for the organisation to be provided either by an individual or by a local institution or even by a single nation. It should have the co-operation, on a world-basis, of specialists in diverse specific subjects. It should therefore be taken up by a world-organisation which can command international co-operation. Unesco is the only world-organisation that can do this. It can utilise international brain-power organised as Ifla and FID, provide its own funds and also attract aid from the industrial organisations of the world and from well-known foundations like those of Carnegie and Rockefeller. It can make available for scrutiny an exhaustive collection of current abstracts and the subject headings used in different establishments, out of which can be distilled the primordial schedules, 120 or 2400 in number as the case may be. It is only in this way that it can set up the vast team-work necessary to examine the foundations of classification, devise enduring elastic foundations, and set up a permanent body to maintain the resulting classification scheme with the necessary continuous improvement. The most favourable place to establish the headquarters for fundamental research in classification is perhaps the Princeton Institute for Fundamental Studies which provides the atmosphere and facilities necessary for basic work of this nature.

INDEX

References are to numbers of parts, chapters and sections

d. i. r. t. = described in relation to
i. r. t. = in relation to
q. i. r. t = quoted in relation to
r. i. r. t. = referred in relation to

T

U